AF882359

Rebuilding after War: Micro-level Determinants of Poverty Reduction in Mozambique

Kenneth R. Simler
Sanjukta Mukherjee
Gabriel L. Dava
Gaurav Datt

RESEARCH REPORT 132

INTERNATIONAL FOOD POLICY RESEARCH INSTITUTE, WASHINGTON, DC

International Food Policy Research Institute
2033 K Street, NW
Washington, DC, 20006-1002 USA
Telephone +1-202-862-5600
www.ifpri.org

Library of Congress Cataloging-in-Publication Data

Rebuilding after war : micro-level determinants of poverty reduction in Mozambique / Kenneth R. Simler . . . [et al.].
p. cm. — (IFPRI research report ; 132)
Includes bibliographical references and indexes.
ISBN 0-89629-135-9 (alk. paper)
1. Economic assistance, Domestic—Mozambique. 2. Poverty—Mozambique. 3. Mozambique—Economic conditions—1975-
I. Simler, Kenneth. II. Research report (International Food Policy Research Institute) ; 132.
HC890.Z9P6365 2003
339.4'6'09679—dc22

2003026935

Contents

Tables

Figures

Foreword

The economic, social, and human costs of war are enormous, and the signing of peace agreements is only the first step in restoring quality of life. In Mozambique the challenge is compounded by the fact that most Mozambicans were impoverished even before the armed struggle for independence (1964–74) and subsequent war against antigovernment rebels (1976–92). Raising living standards is not only beneficial in its own right, but it also helps reduce the likelihood of future conflicts.

Following the country's first multiparty elections in 1994, the government of Mozambique embarked on a program of reconstruction and poverty reduction. National statistical systems had collapsed during the war, so one early priority was to update information about the economy. In 1996 IFPRI began working with the Ministry of Planning and Finance (MPF) and the Eduardo Mondlane University (UEM) to analyze newly collected household and community data to help inform policies to reduce poverty. Close institutional collaboration was fostered in part by having three IFPRI researchers based at MPF and UEM. Research outputs included the country's first comprehensive poverty assessment and numerous other policy analyses focusing on poverty, human capital development, food and nutrition security, and formal and informal safety net programs. This research was also an important building block for the development of Mozambique's Poverty Reduction Strategy.

In this research report, authors Kenneth Simler, Sanjukta Mukherjee, Gabriel Dava, and Gaurav Datt describe the extent and distribution of poverty in Mozambique and analytically examine the factors that determine household living standards and poverty levels. They focus on individual, household, and community characteristics that are not only correlated with poverty, but are also causally linked to poverty outcomes. They develop a microeconometric model to measure the influence of education, employment, demographics, agricultural technology, and infrastructure on household consumption levels. These models are then used in a series of policy simulations to gauge the impact of a range of potential policy interventions to reduce poverty.

The analysis shows that education—including basic literacy and primary education—is an important factor in raising living standards. This is especially true of women's education. Sustained and broad-based economic growth is also necessary to reduce poverty, especially in a country like Mozambique, where two-thirds of the population is below the poverty line. The analysis shows that such growth can be facilitated by increased productivity of smallholder farming and greater investment in infrastructure, particularly in rural areas.

Although the results of this study are most directly useful to policymakers in Mozambique, the analytical methods presented are applicable in many settings. Moreover, the message of reducing poverty through investment in human development as well as physical capital is one that will resonate in many low-income countries.

Joachim von Braun
Director General, IFPRI

Acknowledgments

The analysis presented in this report is part of a larger research project involving collaboration between the Department of Population and Social Development (DPDS, formerly the Poverty Alleviation Unit, and now known as the Department of Macroeconomic Programming) in the National Directorate of Planning and Budget at the Ministry of Planning and Finance, the Faculty of Agronomy and Forestry Engineering at Eduardo Mondlane University (UEM), and the International Food Policy Research Institute (IFPRI). Many individuals and institutions have contributed to the research project and to the production of this report.

The authors thank the Instituto Nacional de Estatística (INE, formerly the Direcção Nacional de Estatística) for providing the data from the 1996–97 Mozambique Inquérito Nacional aos Agregados Familiares Sobre As Condições de Vida (IAF), or National Household Survey of Living Conditions. The authors also appreciate the willingness of the INE staff to accommodate many of their suggestions related to data collection and cleaning. In particular, the authors thank João Dias Loureiro, Manuel da Costa Gaspar, Walter Cavero, and Paulo Mabote from INE. The authors also thank Eugénio Matavel, Cristovão Muahio, and Elísio Mazive of INE for their help with the cleaning of the IAF survey data.

From the Ministry of Planning and Finance (MPF), Government of Mozambique, the authors are grateful to Iolanda Fortes and Vitória Ginja for their sustained support and guidance to the research project. Also from MPF, the authors thank staff from the Gabinete de Estudos for comments and useful discussions at various stages of the project.

From the Faculty of Agronomy and Forestry Engineering, Eduardo Mondlane University, the authors thank Firmino Mucavele for his support of the research project. For comments or other forms of help, the authors also thank Maimuna Ibraimo, Bonifacio José, Cristina Matusse, Gilead Mlay, Patricia Mucavele, João Mutondo, Virgulino Nhate, Farizana Omar, Dimas Sinoia, Emílio Tostão, and Hélder Zavale.

A number of persons provided thoughtful comments and many different forms of support to the work undertaken for this report. Among them, the authors extend thanks to Harold Alderman, Jehan Arulpragasam, Tim Buehrer, Sérgio Cassamo, Jaikishan Desai, Lourdes Fidalgo, James Garrett, Lawrence Haddad, Sudhanshu Handa, Haydee Lemus, John Maluccio, Miguel Mausse, Margaret McEwan, Saul Morris, Diego Rose, Ana Paula Santos, Sumathi Sivasubramanian, Finn Tarp, and Antoinette van Vugt. For additional insightful comments during the research report review process, we thank John Pender, the internal IFPRI reviewer, and two anonymous referees. Their constructive critiques have improved the report considerably.

The authors are particularly grateful to Dean Jolliffe and Jan Low for their valuable contributions, especially at the early stages of work on the research project, which laid the foundation for much of the analytical work undertaken later, including that for this report.

For their suggestions and comments, the authors express thanks to the participants in several seminars organized at the DPDS and the UEM, and at the Conference on Food Security and Nutrition held in Maputo on October 16 and 19, 1998, where results from different stages of research were presented. Although this research was funded by, and carried out in close cooperation with, the government of Mozambique, the views expressed are the authors' and do not represent the official position of the Mozambican government. Any remaining errors are solely the responsibility of the authors.

Summary

A devastating war that lasted from the 1970s to 1992 left the people of Mozambique among the poorest in the world. Since the peace agreement was signed, the government has endeavored to rebuild the country's infrastructure and to improve living standards. Poverty reduction is the primary goal of the government, as well as nongovernmental organizations and donors operating in Mozambique; it is an essential first step to determine the true extent of poverty and where it is most severe. Toward this effort, the International Food Policy Research Institute, the Mozambique Ministry of Planning and Finance, and the Eduardo Mondlane University in Maputo, Mozambique, have jointly undertaken a large research project on the state of poverty in Mozambique. To provide a statistical basis for the research, a National Household Survey of Living Conditions, covering 8,289 households, was conducted in 1996–97 and a report was published in 1998, covering a broad range of topics including poverty, food security, education, nutrition, health, and safety nets. The present report zeroes in on the key question of what determines living standards and poverty in Mozambique, with the aim of identifying those public policy interventions that are likely to reduce poverty the most.

Rather than looking at the association between poverty and various household and individual characteristics on a one-to-one basis (bivariate analysis), which often oversimplifies complex relationships and can lead to erroneous conclusions, this report uses multiple regression to analyze poverty and living standards econometrically. As methodological choices can have a strong influence on the results, much of the report is given over to a detailed discussion of the methodology used to conduct the analysis and sensitivity analysis to assess the robustness of the findings to alternative methodological choices. These include the construction of region-specific poverty lines and the empirical model of poverty determinants used. Estimates of poverty levels and the results of the model are presented, followed by simulations that indicate the impact on poverty of specific policy interventions.

Although the goal is to determine the extent of absolute poverty—a fixed standard of living—in the country as a whole, prices, demographics, and consumption patterns differ from one area to another. Therefore, regional poverty lines are drawn (rather than a single line) in order to approximate a uniform standard of living. By grouping together provinces with similar patterns, 13 regions and 13 food and nonfood poverty lines are devised. The 13 poverty lines reflect regional differences in the cost of attaining the same minimum standard of living.

Per capita consumption (total household consumption divided by the number of household members), rather than income, is used as the basic measure of individual welfare in this report. The consumption measure includes food and nonfood goods and services, whether purchased, home-produced, or received as a gift or payment in kind. Employing a two-step approach, the authors model the determinants of household consumption and then use standard poverty indexes—such as the headcount ratio and the poverty gap—to measure poverty as a function of the household's consumption level and the relevant poverty line.

When the poverty lines are applied to the 1996–97 survey data, it appears that 10.9 million people—two-thirds of the population at that time—lived in a state of absolute poverty, with the incidence of poverty higher in rural than in urban areas. The incidence of poverty is highest in the central part of the country, with poverty rates about the same in the north and the south. At the provincial level, poverty rates varied widely, with slightly less than one-half of the population in Maputo City below the poverty line, rising to 88 percent in Sofala province.

The econometric model of poverty determinants includes demographic data such as age and sex of household members, education levels, employment, landholding, use of agricultural inputs, type of crops cultivated, community characteristics and access to services, and seasonal variations in welfare. As a test of sensitivity to underlying assumptions, alternative models that allowed for different definitions of the poverty lines and the dependent and independent variables were also examined; these produced similar results.

The analysis identifies five principal elements of a poverty reduction strategy for Mozambique. These include (1) increased investment in education, (2) sustained economic growth, (3) adoption of measures to raise agricultural productivity, (4) improved rural infrastructure, and (5) reduced numbers of dependents in households.

The research shows that education is a key determinant of living standards. Even one person in a household with education beyond the primary level tends to boost a family out of poverty. Therefore, high priority should be given to increasing school enrollment and achievement, while also addressing the gender, urban and rural, and regional disparities that currently exist.

During the prolonged period of strife and economic decline, 1987–96, per capita GDP grew at only 0.6 percent a year. With peace, the prospects for economic growth and poverty reduction are promising. A sustained annual growth rate in per capita consumption of 4 percent in real terms over the next five years could reduce the incidence of poverty by as much as 20 percent, if the growth rate is equal across all income levels.

Much of this success in reducing poverty depends on increasing agricultural productivity by promoting the use of modern agricultural inputs such as improved seed varieties, fertilizer, and mechanization. At the time of the survey only a small percentage of Mozambican farmers used improved inputs. In a setting where land availability is not a binding constraint over much of the country, increasing the size of smallholders' land is not likely to reduce poverty significantly. Wider provision of roads, markets, banks, and extension and communication services to rural villages would also go a long way toward stimulating agriculture and reducing poverty.

The research indicates that the larger the number of dependents supported by a working adult, the more likely the household is to fall beneath the poverty line. Family planning programs will not only alleviate poverty but also improve women's health, labor force participation, and productivity. The importance of women's education in this context cannot be overemphasized.

It may not be surprising that the priority areas for development are among those that were most adversely affected by the war: roads, bridges, schools, and teachers were all frequent targets of antigovernment rebels. Nevertheless, even at the low levels found in post-war Mozambique, education, infrastructure, and agricultural technology are key factors that distinguish poorer households from richer households and also point the way to poverty reduction in the future.

CHAPTER 1

Introduction

Mozambique was one of the last countries to emerge from colonial rule in Sub-Saharan Africa. During the more than three centuries of the colonial period, economic development in Mozambique was modest at best (Newitt 1995; Tarp et al. 2002a). Independence from Portugal was attained in 1975, but the colonial period of low investment in economic, social, and human development was followed by a devastating war that began shortly after independence. Although domestic dissent existed, the war was largely driven by outside parties. The Renamo (Resistência Nacional de Moçambique) guerrillas who fought the government were sponsored initially by the white minority government in neighboring Rhodesia. The Rhodesian regime objected to Mozambique providing a haven for Zimbabwe African National Union soldiers who were fighting for majority rule in Rhodesia (now Zimbabwe). After transition to majority rule in Zimbabwe in 1980, Renamo received financial, logistical, and military backing from the apartheid government in South Africa, which was annoyed by Mozambique's support of the liberation movements in that country. Right-wing groups in Portugal and the United States also provided material support to Renamo. Renamo's strategy was based on destabilization, emphasizing sabotage of infrastructure and attacks on schools, health posts, and other development projects.

A peace accord was signed only in 1992, and the first multiparty democratic national elections were held in 1994. Once the war ended, millions of displaced people attempted to resume their normal lives, and the government turned to the task of initiating the process of economic stabilization, recovery, and development. These long, difficult times, however, had serious consequences for the living standards of the population. Thus, in 1997, Mozambique's gross national product (GNP) per capita was estimated to be US$90, the lowest in the world (World Bank 1999). When adjusted for purchasing power parity, Mozambique fared only slightly better, ranking as the 13th poorest country.

After the war, the government of Mozambique undertook many actions to rebuild the infrastructure that had been destroyed or neglected during the war and to improve living standards. The government adopted policies to open the economy and make it more market-oriented, while at the same time attempting to maintain some form of economic and social safety net for the poorest. Although there are signs that these recent efforts to rebuild and reform the economy of Mozambique have resulted in an improvement in general living conditions, a large proportion of the Mozambican population is believed to be living in a state of absolute poverty. Poverty reduction is thus a major objective of the government, as well as of nongovernmental organizations and international donors in Mozambique. The first step in meeting that objective is to find out how much poverty there really is in Mozambique and where it is located.

This report presents an analysis of the determinants of poverty in Mozambique, which is based on nationally representative data from the first national household living standards survey since the end of the war: the Mozambique Inquérito Nacional aos Agregados Familiares Sobre As Condições de Vida (IAF), or National Household Survey of Living Conditions. The report is part of a larger research project on the state of poverty in Mozambique, undertaken jointly by the International Food Policy Research Institute (IFPRI), the Mozambique Ministry of Planning and Finance (MPF), and the Eduardo Mondlane University (UEM) in Maputo. The detailed findings from the work on this project are presented in the report, "Understanding Poverty and Well-Being in Mozambique: The First National Assessment (1996–97)," hereafter referred to as the Mozambique Poverty Assessment Report, or PAR (MPF/UEM/IFPRI 1998). Whereas the PAR covers a wide range of topics, including poverty, food security, nutrition, health, education, and formal and informal safety nets, this report focuses on the key question of the determinants of living standards and poverty in Mozambique.

Motivation for the Research

A useful starting point for an analysis of the determinants of poverty can be a poverty profile. A detailed poverty profile for Mozambique is presented in the PAR, and it serves as an important descriptive tool for examining the characteristics of poverty in the country (MPF/UEM/IFPRI 1998). Poverty profile tables provide key information on the correlates of poverty and hence also provide important clues to the underlying determinants of poverty. However, the tabulations in poverty profiles are typically bivariate in nature, in that they show how poverty levels are correlated with one characteristic at a time. At most, such tables show the association between poverty and two or three other pertinent (usually discrete) characteristics, for example, a table of poverty rates for various occupational classifications, disaggregated by sex and rural or urban area of residence. This tends to limit their usefulness because bivariate comparisons may erroneously simplify complex relationships. For example, when education of the head of the household is compared with poverty status, it is not clear if the observed negative relationship should be attributed to education per se, or to some other factor that might be correlated with education, such as the amount of land held by the household. For this reason, the typical bivariate associations found in a poverty profile can be misleading; they leave unanswered the question of how a particular variable affects poverty *conditional on* the level of other potential determinants of poverty.

There are contexts where unconditional poverty profiles are relevant to a policy decision, as, for instance, in the case of geographical or indicator targeting, but more often, conditional poverty effects are more relevant for evaluating proposed policy interventions that seek to alter only one or a limited set of conditions at a time. In other words, the effect of a policy intervention is correctly identified when one controls for the other potential factors affecting poverty. It is not surprising, therefore, that recent empirical poverty assessments have included econometric analysis of living standards and poverty based upon multiple regression.[1]

While there has been some work on the empirical modeling of the determinants of poverty at the subnational level for Mozambique (such as Sahn and del Ninno's 1994

[1]See, for instance, Glewwe (1991), World Bank (1994a, 1994b, 1995a, 1995b, 1995c, 1996a, 1996b), Grootaert (1997), Dorosh et al. (1998), Datt and Jolliffe (1999), and Mukherjee and Benson (2003).

analysis for Maputo and Matola), to our knowledge there has been no such modeling effort using nationally representative data, or even data with national coverage, because such data did not exist until recently. The completion of the 1996–97 IAF survey alleviated this constraint, and this survey serves as the principal source of data for the analysis presented in this report. This data set is described in Chapter 3.

Structure of this Report

This report is organized as follows. The approach to modeling the determinants of poverty is described in Chapter 2. In Chapter 3, the primary data source is introduced and the approach to the measurement of living standards is discussed. Chapter 4 presents details of the construction of region-specific absolute poverty lines. Estimates of poverty in Mozambique are presented in Chapter 5. In Chapter 6, the empirical model is presented, the set of determinants used in the analysis is introduced, and a number of specification issues are discussed. Chapter 7 presents the results from the estimates of the preferred determinants model. Based on these estimates, in Chapter 8, a number of simulations that indicate the poverty impact of specific policy interventions are presented. Chapter 9 goes beyond the determinants analysis to look at the potential of general economic growth for poverty reduction in Mozambique. Concluding remarks are offered in the final chapter.

CHAPTER 2

Modeling the Determinants of Poverty

Total consumption per capita is used as the welfare measure throughout the subsequent analysis. Its strengths and shortcomings are considered in this chapter. The econometric approach to modeling the determinants of poverty is then examined, including a discussion of the relative merits of estimating poverty measures derived from estimated consumption levels versus estimating the poverty measures directly.

Choice of the Individual Welfare Measure

Throughout this study, we use per capita consumption (that is, total household consumption divided by the number of household members) for the basic measure of individual welfare. Either consumption or income is a defensible measure of welfare as they both measure an individual's ability to obtain goods and services, and both measures should produce fairly similar results for many issues. While we believe that either consumption or income is a useful aggregate money metric (monetary measure) of welfare, we acknowledge that both measures fail to incorporate some important aspects of individual welfare, such as consumption of commodities supplied by, or subsidized by, the public sector (for example, schools, health services, public sewage facilities) and several dimensions of the quality of life (for example, consumption of leisure and the ability to lead a long and healthy life).

The decision to use a consumption-based rather than an income-based measure of individual welfare in this study is motivated by several considerations. First, income can be interpreted as a measure of welfare opportunity, whereas consumption can be interpreted as a measure of welfare achievement (Atkinson 1989). Since not all income is consumed, nor is all consumption financed out of income, the two measures typically differ. Consumption is arguably a more appropriate indicator if we are concerned with realized, rather than potential, welfare. Second, consumption typically fluctuates less than income. Individuals rely on savings, credit, and transfers to smooth the effects of fluctuations in income on their consumption, and therefore consumption provides a more accurate and more stable measure of an individual's welfare over time.[2] Third, some researchers and policymakers hold the belief that survey respondents are more willing to reveal their consumption behavior than they are

[2]Economic theory suggests, for instance, that individuals respond to fluctuations in income streams by saving in good periods and dissaving in lean periods. Even though the permanent income hypothesis is often rejected by available data, households engage in enough consumption smoothing to render consumption a better measure of long-term welfare. This consideration is likely to be even more important for a survey like the IAF, which obtains measures of income and consumption for a given household at only one point in time.

willing to reveal their income.[3] Fourth, in developing countries a relatively large proportion of the labor force is engaged in self-employed activities and measuring income for these individuals is particularly difficult.[4] (See World Bank 1995d for a discussion of the composition of labor forces in developing countries.) Similarly, many individuals are engaged in multiple income-generating activities in a given year, and the process of recalling and aggregating income from different sources is also difficult. (See Reardon 1997 and references therein for more information on household income diversification in Sub-Saharan Africa.)

While consistent with standard practice, the use of per capita normalization of consumption nevertheless also involves a number of assumptions. First, as a welfare measure, per capita normalization effectively implies equal requirements, in monetary terms, for each household member, regardless of age, sex, or other characteristics. But, in the case of food requirements, it is arguable that children's requirements are less than those of adults; the opposite may be true for other goods and services, such as education. Thus consumption is sometimes expressed in adult equivalent units (AEU), whereby children are counted as fractions of adults. A wide range of adult equivalence scales exist, and none are completely satisfactory because they require strong identifying assumptions (see, for example, Deaton and Case 1988 and the excellent review in Deaton 1997). Second, per capita normalization ignores the possibility of economies of scale in household size, for example, the prospect that it is less expensive for two persons to live together than it is for them to live separately. While there is evidence that economies of scale exist, varying largely with consumption patterns within the household, like adult equivalent scales they too require strong assumptions (Lanjouw and Ravallion 1995; Lipton and Ravallion 1995; Deaton 1997; Deaton and Paxson 1998). Third, per capita normalization ignores distribution within the household, although intrahousehold allocation clearly has welfare implications. As there is no universally accepted approach to dealing with the first two issues, we examine the sensitivity of our results to the per capita normalization by adjusting the consumption measure to take into account differential requirements by age and sex and economies of household size. The available data do not permit sensitivity analysis of the third issue, but it has been noted that per capita measures are usually adequate if the objective is to study patterns of poverty, as opposed to targeting of individual households (Haddad and Kanbur 1990).

In this study, we use a comprehensive measure of consumption as the money metric of welfare, drawing upon several modules of the household survey. It measures the total value of consumption of food and nonfood items (including purchases, home-produced items, and gifts received), as well as imputed use values for owner-occupied housing and household durable goods. The only significant omission from the consumption measure is consumption of commodities supplied by the public sector free of charge, or the subsidized element in such

---

[3]A result that lends some support to this conjecture is that household survey data have sometimes found that direct estimates of household savings are greater than savings estimated as income minus consumption. But there also exist examples where the reverse is true. See Kochar 1997 for a discussion of this issue.

[4]For example, one important form of self-employment is working on the household farm, and measuring total net income from farming is both difficult and subject to considerable measurement error. In addition, an annual reference period is needed for adequate estimates of agricultural incomes, which either requires multiple visits to households or longer recall periods, with potentially larger errors.

commodities.[5] For example, an all-weather road, or a public market, or a public water tap presumably enhances the well-being of the people who use those facilities. However, as is true of almost all household surveys, the IAF data do not permit quantification of those benefits, and they are therefore not included in the consumption measure. Further details of the construction of the measure of household consumption are given in Appendix 1.

Approaches to Modeling Poverty Determinants

We can distinguish two main approaches to modeling the determinants of poverty. We now introduce these two approaches, and discuss our reasons for preferring one of them for the current study.

Our preferred approach is to model the determinants of poverty using a two-step procedure. In the first step, we model determinants of the log of consumption at the household level.[6] The simplest form of such a model could be as follows:

$$\ln c_j = \beta' x_j + \varepsilon_j \tag{1}$$

where c_j is consumption of household j (usually on a per capita or per adult equivalent basis), x_j is a set of household characteristics and other determinants, and ε_j is a random error term. The second step defines poverty as a function of the household's consumption level. Here we decided to use the Foster-Greer-Thorbecke class of P_α poverty measures (Foster, Greer, and Thorbecke 1984). Thus, the poverty measure for household j may be written as

$$P_{\alpha,j} = [\max(1 - c_j / z), 0]^\alpha \ , \ \alpha \geq 0 \tag{2}$$

where z denotes the poverty line and α is a nonnegative parameter. The household equivalents of the headcount index, the poverty gap index, and the squared poverty gap index are obtained when α is 0, 1, and 2, respectively. Aggregate poverty for a population, or subpopulation, with n households is simply the mean of this measure across all households, weighted by household size (h_j), giving

$$P_\alpha = \left(\sum_{j=1}^{n} h_j p_{\alpha,j} \right) \Big/ \left(\sum_{j=1}^{n} h_j \right). \tag{3}$$

This approach contrasts with a direct modeling of household-level poverty measures, wherein

$$P_{\alpha,j} = \beta'_\alpha x_j + \eta_{\alpha,j} \tag{4}$$

This direct approach has been used often; see, for example, Bardhan 1984; Gaiha 1988; Sahn and del Ninno 1994; World Bank 1994a, 1995a, 1995b, 1996a, 1996b; and Grootaert 1997. Despite the popularity of this approach, there are several reasons why modeling household consumption may be preferable to modeling household poverty levels.

First, using data on $P_{\alpha j}$ only is inefficient. It involves a loss of information because the information on household living standards above the poverty line is deliberately suppressed (Pudney 1999). All nonpoor households are thus treated alike, as censored data. In the case of the headcount index, all information about the distribution below the poverty line is also suppressed, so that the poor are treated as one homogeneous group and the nonpoor as another homogeneous group.

Second, there is an element of inherent arbitrariness about the exact level of the

[5]Our thanks to an anonymous referee for helping us refine this point.

[6]The logarithm of consumption is used as the dependent variable because its distribution more closely approximates the normal distribution than does the distribution of consumption levels.

absolute poverty line, even if relative differentials in cost of living, as established by the regional poverty lines, are considered robust. Different poverty lines would imply that household consumption data would be censored at different levels. The estimated parameters of the poverty model expressed in equation (4) would therefore change with the level of the poverty line used.[7] As demonstrated by Pudney (1999), there arises a logical inconsistency with modeling poverty as a binary outcome, in that there will be some combinations of household characteristics such that for a range of poverty lines the probability of being poor need not be increasing in the poverty line (that is, the implied cumulative density function is not monotonic). On the other hand, modeling consumption directly has the potentially attractive feature that the consumption model estimates are independent of the poverty line. The link with the household poverty level is established in a subsequent, discrete step. It is worth noting that, once household consumption, c_j, is modeled, the household's poverty level, $P_{\alpha,j}$, is readily determined for any given poverty line z.[8]

Third, estimation of the consumption model avoids strong distributional assumptions that would typically be necessary for nonlinear limited dependent variable models (Powell 1994). A related issue has to do with the number of nonlimit observations, which is directly determined by the observed headcount index for the sample. A low headcount index can seriously constrain the number of nonlimit observations available for estimation.

However, the view that estimating consumption functions is preferable to estimating poverty functions is not universal.[9] There may arguably be occasions when it is appropriate to use data "inefficiently" by estimating equation (4) directly, such as when the "true" consumption function parameters are different for the poor and nonpoor. For example, the nonpoor might not only have higher educational (human capital) levels than the poor, but they might also receive higher returns per unit of education. As the coefficients estimated from model (1) are a weighted average of the poor and nonpoor responses, the estimated coefficient would overstate the consumption-increasing—and poverty-decreasing—effect of increasing educational levels among the poor. In contrast, estimating equation (4) as a Tobit model to accommodate the censoring of the data above the poverty line could possibly better capture the true relationship between education and poverty among the poor.

For a comparison of the two approaches, see Appleton's (2001) study of the determinants of the poverty gap (P_1) in Uganda. Appleton (2001) finds that for most variables, especially human capital and other assets, the two approaches perform equally well. However, most of the ar-

[7]Moreover, when the poverty line is estimated from empirical data, as is done in many studies (using relative poverty lines fixed at a certain proportion of the mean or the median or a certain quantile), the consistency and asymptotic distributions of the logit and probit estimators are not automatically applicable (Pudney 1999).

[8]When working with predicted consumption levels one must also take account of the stochastic element of such predictions. As there is a standard error associated with estimated consumption levels, there is a nonzero probability that a household is nonpoor even if its predicted consumption is less than the poverty line ($\hat{c}_j < z$) and vice versa. Thus, in the case of the poverty headcount, for example, it is appropriate to refer to the prediction ($\hat{P}_{o,j}$) as the probability that a household with given characteristics is below the poverty line. This is discussed in greater detail in the context of the policy simulations presented in Chapter 8.

[9]We would like to thank an anonymous referee for pointing out some of these counterarguments.

guments given for expecting differential returns to characteristics (segmented labor markets, barriers to entry, credit constraints, unobserved household attributes, or nonconvexities in consumption) are essentially arguments about model specification issues related to the inclusion of interaction terms, potentially omitted variables, and functional form. While an attempt ought to be made to address these issues as well as we possibly can with available data (and we endeavor to do that), the arguments in favor of estimating consumption functions are more compelling.

Hence, after considering the advantages and disadvantages of each approach, we decided to model consumption as in equation (1), and then employ equation (2) to make inferences or predictions about poverty levels. The simulations take account of the fact that estimated consumption is a prediction, with an associated standard error. As such, the poverty headcount is not simply the proportion of households whose predicted consumption is below the poverty line. Rather, given the estimated regression parameters, it is the probability that a household will be below the poverty line, conditional on its observable characteristics. This approach is also extended to other poverty measures, namely the poverty gap (P_1) and squared poverty gap (P_2). The methodological details are described in more detail in Chapter 8.

CHAPTER 3

Data

The IAF survey, which provides the data for this study, was designed and implemented by the INE and was conducted from February 1996 through April 1997. The sample consists of 8,289 households and is nationally representative. The survey covered rural and urban areas of all 10 of Mozambique's provinces, plus the city of Maputo as a separate stratum. This survey includes information about consumption patterns, incomes, health, nutrition, education, agriculture, and numerous other aspects of Mozambicans' living conditions.

Overview of the IAF Questionnaire

Each participating household was visited three times within a seven-day period, with three households interviewed per day in rural areas and four households interviewed per day in urban areas. There were three instruments used for household-level interviews: a principal survey questionnaire (Sections 1 through 11), a daily household expenditure questionnaire, and a daily personal expenditure questionnaire administered to all income-earning members within the household.

The principal survey instrument collected information at both individual and household levels. At the individual level, it obtained information for every household member on a broad range of topics, including demographic characteristics, migration history, health, education, and employment status. At the household level, additional information was obtained on landholding size and description, agricultural production during the previous year, livestock ownership, possession of fruit and nut trees, dwelling characteristics, types of basic services used (for example, source of drinking water and type of lighting), asset ownership, major nonfood expenditures during the past three months, regular nonfood expenditures during the past month, transfers into and out of the household, and sources of income. Data collection for both the principal survey and daily expenditures was spread over the three visits to the household to reduce respondent fatigue.

The daily expenditure questionnaire consisted of recall data on major food items and a few typical nonfood items (for example, charcoal and matches) consumed during a seven-day period. During the first interview, recall data from the previous day's consumption were obtained. At the second interview, which was three days after the first interview, consumption data for the days between interviews were collected. At the final interview three days later, recall data on the preceding three days of consumption were obtained.

The same principle of recall data collection was followed for the daily personal expenditure questionnaire. However, one difference was that in the majority of cases for urban workers, the personal diaries were left at the first interview for the income-earning household member to fill out because that person was frequently absent from the household. In practice, many difficulties were encountered in the collection of these data, and because of insufficient compliance, these data suffered from a high (and uneven) nonresponse rate. Therefore, it was decided not to use these data in the construction of the poverty line.[10]

In addition to data collected at individual and household levels, there were two instruments administered once during the survey period at higher levels of aggregation. First, within each village (*aldeia*), a community-level survey of available infrastructure, access to services, and general community characteristics was conducted. These data were not collected in any urban areas. Second, detailed market price information (including weighing all items sold in nonstandard containers) was collected in the major market for each sampled urban area (*bairro*) or rural area (*localidade*).

Sample Design

The sample frame or universe from which the sample was selected covered the population of Mozambique residing in households, and excluded those residing in prisons, army camps, hotels, and so forth. At the time of the survey design, the most recent census data available were from 1980. Given the substantial population growth and movements that had occurred since 1980, a sampling frame based on noncensus data had to be devised. For all areas outside of provincial capitals the most recent information with national coverage was the Electoral Census conducted in preparation for the elections in 1994. However, the electoral census proved unsuitable for larger urban centers where persons were often registered at locations not corresponding to their place of residence. Consequently, an alternative selection methodology was devised for provincial capitals and Maputo City. This methodology is described later in this chapter.

The sample was selected in three stages and geographically stratified to ensure that (1) the entire sample is nationally representative, (2) the urban (rural) sample is representative of urban (rural) households, and (3) each provincial sample is representative at the province level (treating the capital city of Maputo as a separate province). This design allows for analysis at national, provincial, and urban and rural levels. Data collection occurred throughout the year within the rural sample of each province to assure coverage during the different seasons of the year. Table 3.1 presents the temporal distribution of completed interviews; it is organized by the 13 geographic units used to define region-specific poverty lines, as described in Chapter 4.

In the first step of the selection process, the sample consisted of 10 provinces divided into urban and rural strata plus an additional stratum consisting of Maputo City. Administrative divisions for urban areas (from largest to smallest) are *distrito* (district), *bairro* (neighborhood or ward), and *quarteirão* (block). The divisions in rural areas are *distrito, posto administrativo* (administrative post), *localidade* (locality), and *aldeia* (village).

In each of the rural strata, *localidades* were chosen as the primary sampling unit (PSU). Selection was based on probability proportional to size, that is, the estimated population of the *localidade* as a proportion of the total estimated population of the province. Because of limited resources, the survey did not construct its own population lists, but instead relied upon existing population data at the local level for selection of *localidades* and *aldeias*. The process was complicated by the fact that in some *aldeias*, actual population data were avail-

[10]This means working with a somewhat more restricted definition of consumption, which is a less than ideal situation, but arguably better than using a more inclusive but less consistent, and less comparable, measure of consumption.

Table 3.1 Spatial distribution of the sample, by month of interview

Month/year	Niassa and Cabo Delgado		Nampula		Sofala and Zambézia		Manica and Tete		Gaza and Inhambane		Maputo Province		Maputo City	Number of households	Percent of sample
	Rural	Urban	Rural	Urban	Rural	Urban	Rural	Urban	Rural	Urban	Rural	Urban			
February 96	27	36	0	47	26	48	27	25	12	45	0	0	12	305	3.7
March 96	0	36	0	47	66	48	27	47	33	99	0	72	96	571	8.6
April 96	108	0	47	47	97	36	98	24	108	0	0	72	72	709	9.3
May 96	80	72	97	0	98	36	64	83	99	0	0	72	71	772	8.8
June 96	99	71	36	72	91	0	100	0	118	0	0	72	73	732	8.6
July 96	118	0	71	24	144	0	88	0	135	0	53	0	82	715	9.3
August 96	55	0	0	0	75	0	0	0	107	0	18	0	98	353	4.3
September 96	134	0	72	0	123	0	108	0	135	0	37	0	72	681	8.2
October 96	80	0	72	0	116	0	81	0	108	0	54	0	72	583	7.0
November 96	81	0	71	0	155	0	108	0	81	0	27	0	74	597	7.2
December 96	109	0	73	0	98	0	54	34	54	0	54	0	70	546	6.6
January 97	111	0	72	0	72	110	45	36	135	0	54	0	108	743	9.0
February 97	104	0	72	0	48	70	54	0	51	36	81	0	0	516	6.2
March 97	55	0	36	0	60	0	81	36	12	0	48	0	0	328	9.0
April 97	27	0	0	0	36	0	54	0	0	0	6	0	0	123	4.0
Total	1,188	215	719	237	1,305	348	989	285	1,188	180	432	288	900	8,274	100.0
Percent	14.4	2.6	8.7	2.9	15.8	4.2	12	3.4	14.4	2.2	5.2	3.5	10.9	100.0	

Source: Mozambique National Household Survey of Living Conditions, 1996–97.

able; in others, only the number of households was available. Within a given *localidade, aldeias* were selected proportional to total *localidade* population when all *aldeias* had population data. Otherwise, selection procedures were based on the number of households per *aldeia.* In total, three to four *aldeias* were selected within each *localidade,* completing the second stage of sampling.

For the final stage within the rural areas of each province, the survey team constructed a list of all households within the selected *aldeias* and simple random selection procedures were used to choose nine households to be interviewed per village.

In the urban provincial capitals and Maputo City, the PSUs were bairros, which were systematically selected with a probability proportional to size. In this instance, size was not defined in terms of the total number of persons, but on the number of *quarteirões* (blocks) found in each *bairro.* Underlying this selection procedure was the knowledge that in the early post-independence period (1975–80), a *quarteirão* corresponded to 25 households. Therefore, in this selection procedure, an assumption is being made that *quarteirões* are approximately of equal size. In the second stage of sampling, *quarteirões* were selected. The final stage of sample selection in each urban area entailed a simple random selection procedure of 12 households chosen from a list of all households compiled for each *quarteirão* selected.

At the end of the sampling exercise, 8,289 households had been selected, distributed across provinces as shown in Table 3.2 (Cavero 1998). Among the selected households, 8,276 were interviewed and data were entered for 8,274 households. Twenty-four of these households were excluded from the present analysis because of severe problems of incomplete data, leaving a sample of 8,250 households comprising 42,180 individuals. In total, 112 of 128 districts nationwide had households included in the survey (INE 1999). More details on the sample design are in Cavero (1998) and an overview is presented in Figure 3.1.

Table 3.2 Sample distribution, by sampling units and province

	Provincial capitals			Rest of province			Total
Province	Number of *bairros*[a]	Number of *quarteirões*[b]	Number of households	Number of *localidades*[c]	Number of *aldeias*[d]	Number of households	Number of households
Niassa	2	6	72	21	63	585	657
Cabo Delgado	2	6	72	25	75	675	747
Nampula	3	12	144	22	88	816	960
Zambézia	2	8	96	22	88	792	888
Tete	2	6	72	20	60	546	618
Manica	4	12	144	19	57	522	666
Sofala	7	21	252	19	57	513	765
Inhambane	2	6	72	24	72	657	729
Gaza	2	6	72	21	63	567	639
Maputo Province	8	24	288	16	48	432	720
Maputo City	37	75	900	...	...	...	900
National total	71	182	2,184	209	671	6,105	8,289

Source: INE 1999.
[a]*Bairros* are neighborhoods or wards in urban areas.
[b]*Quarteirões* are blocks in urban areas.
[c]*Localidades* are rural localities.
[d]*Aldeias* are villages within a rural locality.

Figure 3.1 Sample design for the Mozambique National Household Survey of Living Conditions, 1996–97.

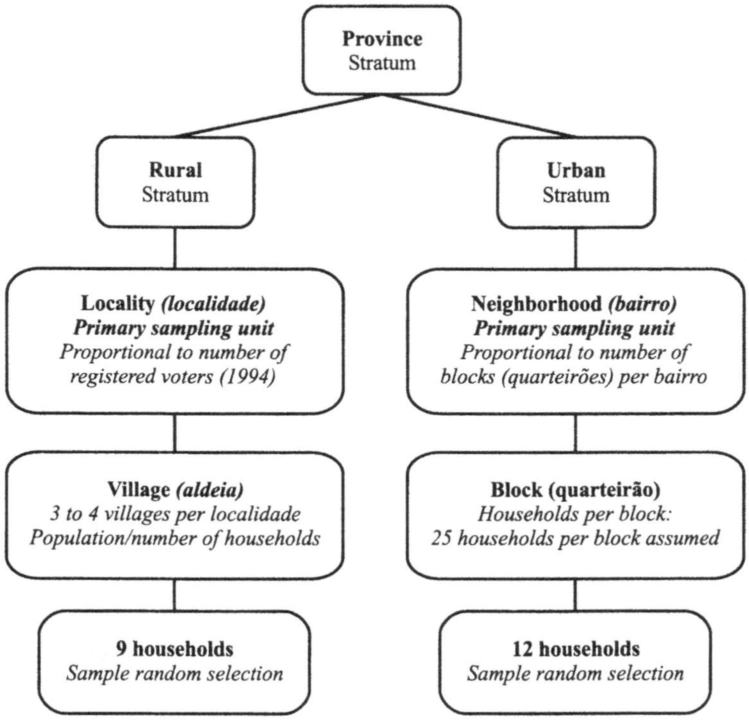

Source: Cavero 1998.

Fieldwork

Work related to sample design began in June 1995. Training of survey interviewers and supervisors took place during a two-week period in November 1995, with pilot testing of the questionnaire occurring in December 1995 and January 1996. Field manuals with instructions for interviewers, field supervisors, and provincial-level supervisors were developed along with documentation concerning concepts and definitions used in the survey and codebooks for all survey instruments. These are available in Cavero (1998). For each of the 10 provinces, plus the city of Maputo, there was a team consisting of the provincial supervisor (an INE permanent employee), the field supervisor, three household interviewers, one anthropometrist (for measuring children), and one market enumerator (for community price data).

Data collection at the household level in the field started in February 1996 and continued through April 1997. Collection of price data in each *bairro* or *localidade* began in October 1996 and was completed in March 1997. Collection of community-level data on infrastructure was completed in October 1997. All data were digitized at INE headquarters in Maputo. Data entry began concurrent with data collection, with all data entered using the Integrated Microcomputer Processing System software package developed and distributed by the United States Census Bureau. All data were entered once, with data entry programs incorporating range checks to reduce data entry errors. One exception to this process is the price data, which were double-entered.

CHAPTER 4

Poverty Lines

In this report, we are concerned with absolute poverty, by which we mean the poverty line is fixed in terms of the standard of living it commands for the area or the domain over which poverty is measured. As we will be concerned with measurement of poverty in Mozambique as a whole, our domain is the entire country. However, prices (both relative prices and price levels), household demographics (and therefore, the basic needs of the household), and consumption patterns differ across regions of the country, and hence a single poverty line in nominal terms for Mozambique as a whole would typically support different standards of living across regions. Thus, to measure absolute poverty consistently, we need a set of region-specific poverty lines, varying in nominal money metric terms, which approximate a uniform standard of living. A detailed discussion of the construction of poverty lines follows.

Cost of Basic Needs Approach

There can be a number of different approaches to the determination of poverty lines. In this study, we follow the cost of basic needs methodology to construct region-specific poverty lines (Ravallion 1994, 1998).[11] By this approach, the total poverty line is constructed as the sum of a food and a nonfood poverty line. Like any poverty lines, the food and nonfood poverty lines embody value judgments on basic food and nonfood needs, and are set in terms of a level of per capita consumption expenditure that is deemed consistent with meeting these basic needs. The following discussion on the derivation of the poverty lines is organized into four main parts dealing, respectively, with (1) identification of regions for the definition of poverty lines, (2) steps in the construction of the food poverty lines, (3) construction of the nonfood poverty lines, and (4) construction of the total region-specific poverty lines and the spatial cost-of-living indexes implied by them.

Identifying Regions for Defining Poverty Lines

It is useful to recall here that our primary interest is in examining absolute poverty and hence we would like to ensure that our poverty line implies a fixed standard of living over the full

[11]Ravallion (1994, 1998) and Ravallion and Bidani (1994), among others, have shown that the cost of basic needs approach does not suffer from the problem of inconsistent poverty comparisons that often arise when the food energy intake method is used to set poverty lines. Using the 1996–97 IAF data, Tarp et al. (2002b) have shown that the food energy intake approach yields inconsistent poverty lines and estimates for Mozambique.

domain of poverty measurement. However, a single poverty line in nominal terms for the whole country will almost surely command different standards of living across regions—most important because prices vary across regions, especially in a country such as Mozambique, where markets are often not spatially integrated and regional price differentials can be large.

It can also be argued that regional differences in household composition and consumption patterns should also be allowed for in the determination of poverty lines. Starting from a uniform set of age- and sex-specific caloric requirements, differences in household composition translate directly into differences in caloric requirements. Similarly (from a more welfarist perspective), to the extent that consumption patterns vary because of regional differences in relative prices, differences in consumption patterns should be taken into account in the assessment of cost-of-living differentials. Thus, an important first step is to define an appropriate level of spatial disaggregation for the construction of poverty lines.

In defining the spatial groupings, or regions, for constructing separate poverty lines, the following three considerations are considered important. First, we want to maintain a rural–urban distinction in the regional definitions because of existing evidence that prices and consumption patterns of the poor vary systematically between urban and rural areas. Second, to avoid problems with small subsample sizes, we want to ensure a minimum of about 150 households for each poverty line region. Third, we want to group those provinces together that are believed to be relatively homogeneous in terms of prices, household composition, and consumption patterns. The second consideration suggests that disaggregating by both rural or urban zone and province was not a feasible option, for it yields subsamples in the urban portions of Cabo Delgado, Zambézia, Tete, Inhambane, and Gaza provinces that are each less than 150 households. Thus, we aggregate over provinces to form the 13 regions shown in Table 4.1. The minimum sample size for a region is 179 for urban Gaza and Inhambane; the maximum sample size is 1,301 for rural Sofala and Zambézia.

Food Poverty Line

As noted above, under the cost of basic needs approach, food poverty lines are tied to the notion of basic food needs, which, in turn, are typically anchored to minimum energy requirements.[12] For each poverty line region, the food poverty line is constructed by determining the food energy (caloric) intake requirements for the reference population (the poor), the caloric content of the typical diet of the poor in that region, and the average cost (at local prices) of a calorie when consuming that diet. The food poverty line—expressed in monetary cost per person per day—is then calculated as the product of the average daily per capita caloric requirement and the average price per composite calorie. Put differently, the food poverty line is the region-specific cost of meeting the minimum caloric requirements when consuming the average food bundle that the poor in that poverty line

[12]It is well understood and appreciated that food energy is only one facet of human nutrition, and that adequate consumption of other nutrients, such as protein, iron, vitamin A, and so forth, is also essential for a healthy and active life. However, like most multipurpose household surveys, the information on food consumption in the IAF data set is not sufficiently detailed to permit estimation of the intake and absorption of other nutrients. Use of energy requirements alone is also well established in the poverty measurement literature (Greer and Thorbecke 1986; Ravallion 1994, 1998; Deaton 1997).

Table 4.1 Distribution of sample households, by poverty line regions

Poverty line region	Number of households	Percent of total sample
Niassa and Cabo Delgado—rural	1,186	14.4
Niassa and Cabo Delgado—urban	214	2.6
Nampula—rural	719	8.7
Nampula—urban	236	2.9
Sofala and Zambézia—rural	1,301	15.8
Sofala and Zambézia—urban	345	4.2
Manica and Tete—rural	987	12.0
Manica and Tete—urban	285	3.5
Gaza and Inhambane—rural	1,187	14.4
Gaza and Inhambane—urban	179	2.2
Maputo Province—rural	431	5.2
Maputo Province—urban	287	3.5
Maputo City	893	10.8
Total	8,250	100.0

Source: Mozambique National Household Survey of Living Conditions, 1996–97.
Note: The poverty line regions are those regions used to construct separate poverty lines, thereby partially controlling for spatial differences in prices and household composition.

region actually consume.[13] It is easy to show that the two notions of the food poverty line are equivalent so long as the average price per calorie is determined using the same reference food bundle.

Minimum Caloric Requirements

The estimated per capita caloric requirement in each poverty line region depends on the average household characteristics of the reference sample in that region. For example, a region with a greater proportion of children in the population will require fewer calories per capita than a region with a higher proportion of middle-aged adults, as children typically have lower caloric requirements.

In principle, when calculating caloric requirements, one needs to take into account an individual's age, sex, body size and composition, physical activity level (PAL), and, for women, whether they are pregnant or in the first six months of breast feeding. As the IAF does not include adequate data on physical activity levels or adult body size and composition,[14] we estimated caloric requirements using the available variables: age, sex, pregnancy status,[15]

[13]The typical food bundle of the poor may, of course, contain more or less calories than the requirement for that region (in Mozambique, it is usually less). This bundle is then proportionally scaled up or down until it yields exactly the preestablished caloric requirement, and the cost of this rescaled bundle at region-specific prices determines the food poverty line for that region.

[14]For all adults we assumed moderate physical activity levels, which, in fact, could represent an infinite number of combinations of PAL and body mass. For example, the 3,000 calories for adult males aged 18 to 30 shown in Table 4.2 could represent the requirements of a 90-kilogram male with a PAL of 1.45, a 50-kilogram male with a PAL of 2.08, or any number of combinations of body mass and PAL.

[15]Although WHO indicates an additional requirement of 285 kilocalories per day in the last trimester of pregnancy, we do not have data on the stage of a woman's pregnancy. As pregnancies in Mozambique are not usually reported until at least the first trimester is completed, we assumed that half of the women who reported pregnancies were in the last trimester.

Table 4.2 Estimated caloric requirements, by age and sex

	Daily caloric requirement	
Age category	Females	Males
Up to 1 year old	820	820
1–2 years old	1,150	1,150
2–3 years old	1,350	1,350
3–5 years old	1,550	1,550
5–7 years old	1,750	1,850
7–10 years old	1,800	2,100
10–12 years old	1,950	2,200
12–14 years old	2,100	2,400
14–16 years old	2,150	2,650
16–18 years old	2,150	2,850
18–30 years old	2,100	3,000
30–60 years old	2,150	2,900
60 years and older	1,950	2,450

Source: WHO 1985.

Notes: An additional 285 calories per day are required for women in the last trimester of pregnancy. An additional 500 calories per day are required by women who are in the first six months of lactation. Adult caloric requirements assume a moderate amount of physical activity.

and breastfeeding status.[16] We began with the age- and sex-specific caloric requirements reported by the World Health Organization (WHO)(1985), presented in Table 4.2. The requirements range from 820 kilocalories per day for children less than one year old to 3,000 kilocalories per day for males between the ages of 18 and 30.

We use the demographic information in the IAF to calculate the average household composition within each poverty line region. We then map the average number of persons in each requirements category (Table 4.2) to the number of kilocalories required, to arrive at an average caloric requirement per household and per capita in each poverty line region. The average per capita caloric requirement in each of the regions is approximately 2,150 kilocalories per day, with a narrow range of 2,114 to 2,217 kilocalories per capita (Table 4.3).[17]

To convert the physical quantities of household food consumption in grams to kilocalories, a number of different sources were used. As all of the sources contain information on some of the same basic food items, such as staple grains, and some of these sources have slightly conflicting

[16]We did not have data indicating how long an individual woman had been breastfeeding her child. However, we did have data on children's ages and whether or not a child was breastfeeding. Thus, we assumed that for each child in the household who was breastfeeding, there was one woman nursing that child; if that child was six months old or less, the mother (and household) was assumed to require the additional 500 kilocalories daily indicated by WHO. Our method overestimates calorie requirements to the extent that multiple births (for example, twins) occur and multiple infants survive the first six months.

[17]The WHO calorie requirements could also be used to construct adult equivalency scales (with respect to calorie requirements). For example, if one takes the maximum requirement (3,000 kilocalories per day for males aged 18 to 30 years) as the base, representing 1.00 AEU, a woman in the same age category would have an AEU of 0.70, or 0.795 if she were in the last trimester of pregnancy, or 0.867 if she were in the first six months of breastfeeding. Likewise, the average AEU per capita in Mozambique is about 0.717.

Table 4.3 Mean daily caloric requirements per capita, mean price per calorie, and food poverty lines

Poverty line region	Mean per capita daily caloric requirements	Mean price per calorie (meticais/calorie)	Food poverty line (meticais/person/day)
Niassa and Cabo Delgado—rural	2,158.70	1.3950	3,011.47
Niassa and Cabo Delgado—urban	2,121.89	1.7375	3,686.83
Nampula—rural	2,162.53	1.2680	2,742.00
Nampula—urban	2,140.38	1.7017	3,642.28
Sofala and Zambézia—rural	2,173.63	1.7109	3,718.80
Sofala and Zambézia—urban	2,173.73	2.4703	5,369.80
Manica and Tete—rural	2,113.97	1.8190	3,845.31
Manica and Tete—urban	2,166.51	2.5610	5,548.39
Gaza and Inhambane—rural	2,142.28	2.3205	4,971.20
Gaza and Inhambane—urban	2,167.12	2.6367	5,713.96
Maputo Province—rural	2,122.04	2.5532	5,418.00
Maputo Province—urban	2,165.39	2.7926	6,047.09
Maputo City	2,217.34	2.7926	6,192.15

Source: Mozambique National Household Survey of Living Conditions, 1996–97.

values for the caloric content of specific items (because of differences in the food item itself, measurement differences, or other reasons), it was necessary to establish a preference ordering for the different sources. The sources used were, in decreasing order of preference, the Mozambique Ministry of Health (Ministério da Saúde 1991); a food table for Tanzania compiled by the University of Wageningen (West, Pepping, and Temalilwa 1988); an East, Central, and Southern Africa food table (West et al. 1987); the U.S. Department of Agriculture food composition database (USDA 1998); the U.S. Department of Health, Education, and Welfare (USHEW 1968); and food composition tables from the University of California at Berkeley.[18]

Reference Food Bundles and the Average Price Per Calorie

An estimate of the average price per calorie for any region can be derived from the total cost of the food bundle typically consumed by the poor in that region and the total calories contained in that bundle. Thus, to compute an average price per calorie for a region, it is necessary to use a reference food bundle. After experimenting with several alternative definitions of the "relatively poor,"[19] we chose to define the relatively poor as those households whose per capita calorie consumption was less than the per capita caloric requirement for their poverty line region. Using this set of relatively poor households, we first calculated the price per calorie paid by each household as the ratio

[18]For further discussion of the factors relevant to establishing a preference ordering of food table sources, see MPF/UEM/IFPRI 1998.

[19]For details, see MPF/UEM/IFPRI 1998.

of its food expenditure to its caloric intake, and then took a weighted average of price per calorie across households within each poverty line region. The weights used are the household's caloric intake multiplied by its survey sampling weight.[20] Thus the composition of the reference food bundles varies across regions,[21] and it bears emphasizing that these bundles are derived from the actual food consumption patterns of poor households in each poverty line region, as captured by the IAF survey.

This weighted average was calculated after imposing a 5 percent trim on the full sample. That is, household-level observations on the mean price per calorie that were below the 5th percentile or above the 95th percentile were excluded from the calculation of the regional level mean price per calorie. This restriction was necessary because of several extreme values of average price per calorie observed at the household level. The extreme values are largely attributable to errors in recording the physical quantity of the food (whether in local or standard units), or the imperfect methods used to convert from nonstandard to standard units. This trim was only applied for the purpose of constructing the average price per calorie and did not require exclusion of these households from other parts of the analysis.

The 13 food poverty lines were calculated by multiplying the mean price per calorie in each poverty line region by the average per capita caloric requirements in that region (Table 4.3). Because the per capita caloric requirements are quite similar across the regions, the variation in the food poverty lines results primarily from variations in the mean cost of a calorie in each region. The food poverty lines, therefore, show the same pattern as the average price per calorie: within a provincial grouping, urban food poverty lines are higher than rural, and the food poverty lines tend to decrease as one moves from south to north.

In mainstream economic analysis of poverty, the composition of the cost of basic needs (CBN) food bundle is usually held fixed across regions, with any variation in the food poverty lines attributable entirely to regional differences in the prices of the bundle components.[22] The use of a fixed bundle is typically justified by the argument that it is necessary to assure that the food poverty lines represent equal levels of welfare. However, if the relative prices of food vary regionally, the comparability of welfare levels across regions is only an illusion, and the fixed bundle CBN method can generate inconsistent poverty comparisons, as demonstrated by Tarp et al. (2002b). Tarp et al. (2002b) find that in Mozambique, large differences in relative prices across regions lead to very different food consumption patterns among poor households, as households substitute toward the foods that are priced lower in their own region. Use of a common bundle across all regions in gen-

[20]Survey sampling weights, sometimes called expansion factors, are equal to the reciprocal of the probability that a household was selected in the sample. The weights are applied to make the survey data representative of the population at the time of the survey, in cases where the probability of selection is not uniform (for example, oversampling of urban households, stratified samples with differential sampling rates, and so on). Further details are available in Cavero 1998.

[21]For the food consumption bundles underlying these mean prices per calorie for the poor in each of the 13 regions, and related details, see MPF/UEM/IFPRI 1998.

[22]The few exceptions to this practice that we are aware of include Lanjouw (1994); Datt, Jolliffe, and Sharma (2001); Mukherjee and Benson (2003); Jolliffe, Datt, and Sharma (2003); and Gibson and Rozelle (2003). Ravallion (1998) also provides conceptual arguments in favor of region-specific basic needs food bundles.

eral leads to higher poverty lines, higher poverty levels, and some reranking in poverty comparisons.

Nonfood Poverty Lines

Whereas the food poverty lines are anchored on physiological needs, no similar basis is readily available for defining nonfood needs. Yet, even very poor households in virtually all settings allocate a nontrivial proportion of their total consumption to nonfood items. Thus, a plausible way of assessing basic nonfood needs is to look at how much households who are barely in a position to meet their food needs spend on nonfood items. This is the approach we use in this study.[23]

The nonfood poverty line is derived by examining the nonfood consumption among those households whose total expenditure is equal to the food poverty line (Ravallion 1994, 1998; Ravallion and Bidani 1994). The rationale is that if a household's total consumption is only sufficient to purchase the minimum amount of calories using a food bundle typical for the poor, any expenditure on nonfoods is either displacing food expenditure or forcing the household to buy a food bundle that is inferior to that normally consumed by the poor, or both. In either case, the nonfood consumption of such a household displaces "essential" food consumption. Hence, such nonfood consumption itself can be considered "essential" or "basic."

It is, of course, highly improbable that any particular household in the sample has a level of total consumption per capita that exactly equals the food poverty line. Even if such a household did exist, it would not be reasonable to base the nonfood poverty line solely on a single household's consumption pattern. Therefore, we instead examine households whose per capita total consumption is in the neighborhood of the food poverty line, with the neighborhood defined as 80 to 120 percent of the food poverty line. Using these households, the cost of the minimum nonfood bundle, z^N, is then estimated nonparametrically as the weighted average nonfood expenditure. In constructing the average, observations closer to the food poverty line, z^F, are given a higher weight, using a kernel estimation with triangular weights (Hardle 1990; Datt, Jolliffe, and Sharma 2001). For example, households whose consumption is within 18 to 20 percent of the food poverty line are given a weight of one, households between 16 to 18 percent of the food poverty line receive a weight of two, and so forth, with the households within 2 percent of the food poverty line receiving a weight of 10. We then proceed to calculate the weighted average nonfood consumption per capita in each of the 13 poverty line regions, weighting household-level observations by the product of the triangular kernel weights, the household expansion factor, and household size.

Table 4.4 presents the nonfood and food poverty lines, as well as the total poverty line, which is obtained as their sum.

Spatial Cost-of-Living Indexes

The 13 poverty lines in Table 4.4 reflect regional differences in the cost of attaining the same minimum standard of living, and the ratios of poverty lines can therefore be considered as spatial cost-of-living indexes for Mozambique. In addition to listing the

[23]For details of an alternative approach that permits a more generous basic nonfood allowance, see Ravallion (1994) and MPF/UEM/IFPRI (1998).

Table 4.4 Food, nonfood, and total poverty lines, and spatial price index

Poverty line region	Food poverty line	Nonfood poverty line	Total poverty line	Spatial price index
Niassa and Cabo Delgado—rural	3,011.47	1,011.24	4,022.71	0.74
Niassa and Cabo Delgado—urban	3,686.83	1,747.53	5,434.36	1.00
Nampula—rural	2,742.00	617.17	3,359.16	0.62
Nampula—urban	3,642.28	1,306.57	4,948.86	0.91
Sofala and Zambézia—rural	3,718.80	1,134.75	4,853.55	0.89
Sofala and Zambézia—urban	5,369.80	2,230.26	7,600.06	1.40
Manica and Tete—rural	3,845.31	868.07	4,713.38	0.87
Manica and Tete—urban	5,548.39	1,865.99	7,414.38	1.36
Gaza and Inhambane—rural	4,971.20	1,461.70	6,432.90	1.18
Gaza and Inhambane—urban	5,713.96	2,112.79	7,826.75	1.44
Maputo Province—rural	5,418.00	1,898.18	7,316.17	1.35
Maputo Province—urban	6,047.09	2,666.80	8,713.89	1.60
Maputo City	6,192.15	2,349.33	8,541.48	1.57

Source: Mozambique National Household Survey of Living Conditions, 1996–97.

food, nonfood, and total poverty lines, Table 4.4 also lists the (normalized) spatial cost-of-living index implied by the 13 total poverty lines.[24] Like the poverty lines, the spatial cost-of-living indexes reflect differences in prices for basic commodities, household composition, and consumption patterns among the relatively poor. It is these spatial cost-of-living indexes that are used to map the nominal values of per capita consumption to comparable values in real terms for defining the dependent variable for estimating the model shown in equation (1).

[24]National average prices are used as the base for normalization. This normalization ensures that the national average nominal total consumption is equal to the national average total consumption adjusted by the spatial cost-of-living index.

CHAPTER 5

Poverty in Mozambique: Estimates for 1996–97

Before discussing the details of the empirical model of the determinants of poverty, it is instructive to look at the estimates of real mean consumption and absolute poverty obtained using the set of poverty lines described in the previous chapter. The 1996–97 IAF survey data indicate that real mean monthly consumption in Mozambique is 160,780 meticais (MT) per person. This is equal to about US$170 per person per year at the average exchange rate prevailing during the survey period.[25] Using the poverty lines derived earlier, the national poverty rate (headcount ratio) is 0.694, indicating that in 1996–97, just over two-thirds of the Mozambican population, or 10.9 million people, lived in a state of absolute poverty. The national average poverty gap index and squared poverty gap index are also high, at 0.293 and 0.156, respectively (see Table 5.1 for details).

The incidence of poverty is higher in rural areas than in urban areas (Table 5.1), with the rural headcount index reaching 0.712, compared with 0.620 in urban areas. The depth and severity of poverty is also higher in rural areas than in urban areas, although only the difference in head count is statistically significant at the 95 percent level. Poverty in Mozambique is predominantly a rural phenomenon. About 82 percent of the poor live in rural areas; this is slightly higher than the share of rural population in total population.[26] Turning to the regional disaggregation, we see that the incidence of poverty is highest in the central region, with the highest values for all three poverty measures, whereas the northern and southern regions are nearly equal in terms of the three poverty measures used. For all three measures, the higher poverty rates in the central region are statistically significant, whereas there is no significant difference between the northern and the southern regions for any of the three. However, if Maputo City—which has the lowest poverty rates in the country—is excluded from the southern

[25]The estimate from the IAF data is considerably higher than other estimates of average individual well-being in Mozambique, such as the US$90 GNP per capita reported by the World Bank (1999). Reports using more recent data (for example, INE 1998) are consistent with our estimates, and it is now generally acknowledged that GDP per capita was underestimated in the early and mid-1990s.

[26]Shortly after completion of the IAF in 1997, Mozambique conducted its second national housing and population census, the first census since 1980. For the census (and subsequent surveys in Mozambique), the definition of urban areas was expanded, which enlarged the share of the population in urban areas from 18 to 30 percent.

Table 5.1 Mean consumption and poverty estimates, by zone and region

Region	Population share (%)	Mean consumption (meticais/ person/month)[a]	Headcount index	Poverty gap index	Squared poverty gap index
Rural	79.7	150,074	0.712	0.299	0.159
		(3,313.2)	(0.012)	(0.008)	(0.006)
Urban[b]	20.3	202,685	0.620	0.267	0.146
		(10,628.7)	(0.027)	(0.018)	(0.014)
Northern[c]	32.5	167,834	0.663	0.266	0.138
		(6,275.2)	(0.023)	(0.015)	(0.011)
Central[c]	42.6	141,990	0.738	0.327	0.180
		(4,470.5)	(0.016)	(0.118)	(0.009)
Southern (including Maputo City)[c]	24.9	183,718	0.658	0.268	0.139
		(7,291.9)	(0.020)	(0.012)	(0.009)
Southern (excluding Maputo City)[c]	18.8	161,036	0.717	0.302	0.159
		(8,381.6)	(0.024)	(0.016)	(0.011)
National	100.0	160,780	0.694	0.293	0.156
		(3,460.8)	(0.011)	(0.008)	(0.006)

Source: Mozambique National Household Survey of Living Conditions, 1996–97.

Notes: Standard errors are in parentheses, corrected for sample design effects.

[a]Mean total consumption, temporally and spatially deflated, using national average prices as the base. (See Chapter 4 and Appendix 1 for details.)

[b]Urban areas include Maputo City, provincial capitals, and small urban centers.

[c]Northern includes Cabo Delgado, Nampula, and Niassa provinces; Central includes Manica, Sofala, Tete, and Zambézia provinces; Southern includes Gaza, Inhambane, and Maputo provinces, plus Maputo City.

region, the remainder of the southern region has poverty rates higher than the northern region and is not significantly different from the central region.

Given that more than two out of every three Mozambicans live below the reference poverty line, there is a case for distinguishing those who are ultrapoor, to help us focus on the poorest among the poor. Although there are many ways to define ultrapoverty, all are admittedly somewhat ad hoc in nature. For the analysis presented here, we set the ultrapoverty line at 60 percent of the total reference poverty line.[27]

Using the 60 percent ultrapoverty line, we estimate that 37.8 percent of the Mozambican population is ultrapoor (Table 5.2). Focusing on this subset of the poor, however, does not yield any particularly new insights at this level of aggregation. Like poverty, the incidence, depth, and severity[28] of ultrapoverty are greatest in

[27]We also experimented with an alternative ultrapoverty line that was set at the food poverty line itself. This line is higher than the 60 percent ultrapoverty line, as the weighted average of food poverty lines is about 76 percent of the reference poverty line. The patterns emerging from this alternative poverty line were not significantly different than those found with either the full reference poverty line or the ultrapoverty line defined as 60 percent of the full poverty line.

[28]The results on severity are not presented in Table 5.2, but are available from the authors.

Table 5.2 Estimates of ultrapoverty, using ultrapoverty lines at 60 percent of the reference poverty line

Region	Headcount index	Poverty gap index	Distribution of the ultrapoor (%)
Rural	0.388	0.120	81.8
	(0.015)	(0.006)	(2.03)
Urban[a]	0.338	0.113	18.2
	(0.030)	(0.015)	(2.03)
Northern[b]	0.341	0.103	29.3
	(0.024)	(0.011)	(2.30)
Central[b]	0.429	0.141	48.4
	(0.022)	(0.010)	(2.54)
Southern (including Maputo City)[b]	0.337	0.103	22.3
	(0.021)	(0.009)	(1.56)
Southern (excluding Maputo City)[b]	0.392	0.120	19.5
	(0.027)	(0.012)	(1.43)
National	0.378	0.119	100.0
	(0.013)	(0.006)	

Source: Mozambique National Household Survey of Living Conditions, 1996–97.
Notes: Standard errors are in parentheses, corrected for sample design effects.
[a]Urban areas include Maputo City, provincial capitals, and small urban centers.
[b]Northern includes Cabo Delgado, Nampula, and Niassa provinces; Central includes Manica, Sofala, Tete, and Zambézia provinces; Southern includes Gaza, Inhambane, and Maputo provinces and Maputo City.

rural areas and in the central region. In fact, the regional patterns are similar with regard to the ranking of the regions and the statistical significance of the differences shown. We note, however, that none of the urban/rural differences in ultrapoverty are statistically significant, whereas the rural headcount is significantly higher when the full reference poverty line is used. When the 60 percent poverty line is used as a measure of ultrapoverty, a greater proportion of the rural population falls below the line than the urban population share, but, on average, the urban ultrapoor have a slightly greater gap between their consumption levels and the ultrapoverty line and greater inequality among the ultrapoor.

Regional differences in poverty and welfare have been a frequent issue in post-independence Mozambique. Turning to Table 5.3, we see significant disparities in mean consumption and poverty measures when the data are disaggregated to the provincial level. The poverty headcount index ranges from a low of 0.478 in Maputo City to a high of 0.879 in Sofala Province. Other provinces with particularly high poverty incidence are Inhambane (0.826) and Tete (0.823), all far above the next poorest province (Niassa, 0.706). The wide variation within regions is particularly striking. For example, note the contrast between Cabo Delgado and Niassa in the north, Manica and Sofala in the center, and Maputo City and Inhambane in the south. The ordinal ranking of the provinces changes very little among the three poverty measures, and given the magnitude of the standard errors, most of the changes in rank are not statistically significant. The most interesting finding along these lines is the comparison between Maputo Province and neighboring Gaza. The two provinces have similar headcount indexes, but Maputo Province's average poverty gap and squared poverty gap measures are considerably higher than Gaza's, indicating more unequal and, on average, lower incomes among the poor in Maputo Province. When considering ultrapoverty, Table 5.4 shows that the distribution of ultrapoverty by province is similar to the distribution of poverty by province, as shown in Table 5.3. Of particular note is the extremely high ultrapoverty headcount in Sofala Province (0.652).

Table 5.3 Mean consumption and poverty estimates, by province

Province	Population share (%)	Mean consumption (meticais/ person/month)[a]	Headcount index	Poverty gap index	Squared poverty gap index
Niassa	4.85	147,841	0.706	0.301	0.161
		(10,787.9)	(0.038)	(0.031)	(0.022)
Cabo Delgado	8.16	194,448	0.574	0.198	0.091
		(12,653.3)	(0.042)	(0.023)	(0.014)
Nampula	19.47	161,668	0.689	0.286	0.153
		(8,743.9)	(0.033)	(0.022)	(0.016)
Zambézia	20.34	154,832	0.681	0.260	0.123
		(6,321.1)	(0.026)	(0.018)	(0.012)
Tete	7.30	117,049	0.823	0.390	0.225
		(8,109.6)	(0.032)	(0.029)	(0.021)
Manica	6.19	191,608	0.626	0.242	0.117
		(22,527.9)	(0.060)	(0.031)	(0.017)
Sofala	8.77	97,906	0.879	0.492	0.320
		(5,807.8)	(0.015)	(0.027)	(0.027)
Inhambane	7.06	128,219	0.826	0.386	0.214
		(10,909.1)	(0.024)	(0.022)	(0.017)
Gaza	6.57	183,233	0.647	0.230	0.109
		(10,828.2)	(0.033)	(0.025)	(0.019)
Maputo Province	5.14	177,774	0.656	0.278	0.147
		(18,642.3)	(0.054)	(0.032)	(0.020)
Maputo City	6.14	253,102	0.478	0.165	0.077
		(21,335.7)	(0.041)	(0.020)	(0.012)

Source: Mozambique National Household Survey of Living Conditions, 1996–97.

Notes: Standard errors are in parentheses, corrected for sample design effects.

[a]Mean total consumption, temporally and spatially deflated, using national average prices as the base.

Table 5.4 Mean consumption and ultrapoverty estimates, by province

Province	Population share (%)	Mean consumption (meticais/ person/month)[a]	Headcount index	Poverty gap index	Squared poverty gap index
Niassa	4.85	147,841	0.405	0.124	0.053
		(10,787.9)	(0.053)	(0.022)	(0.012)
Cabo Delgado	8.16	194,448	0.231	0.060	0.021
		(12,653.3)	(0.038)	(0.012)	(0.004)
Nampula	19.47	161,668	0.371	0.116	0.052
		(8,743.9)	(0.034)	(0.018)	(0.011)
Zambézia	20.34	154,832	0.344	0.078	0.026
		(6,321.1)	(0.039)	(0.012)	(0.005)
Tete	7.30	117,049	0.536	0.187	0.088
		(6,740.0)	(0.040)	(0.020)	(0.011)
Manica	6.19	191,608	0.270	0.075	0.030
		(22,527.9)	(0.038)	(0.016)	(0.008)
Sofala	8.77	97,906	0.652	0.293	0.165
		(5,807.8)	(0.039)	(0.031)	(0.024)
Inhambane	7.06	128,219	0.537	0.172	0.072
		(10,909.1)	(0.038)	(0.020)	(0.011)
Gaza	6.57	183,233	0.265	0.073	0.030
		(10,828.2)	(0.042)	(0.019)	(0.011)
Maputo Province	5.14	177,774	0.354	0.111	0.047
		(18,642.3)	(0.055)	(0.019)	(0.008)
Maputo City	6.14	253,102	0.170	0.048	0.021
		(21,335.7)	(0.022)	(0.010)	(0.007)

Source: Mozambique National Household Survey of Living Conditions, 1996–97.

Notes: The ultrapoverty line is set at 60 percent of the reference poverty line. Standard errors are in parentheses, corrected for sample design effects.

[a]Mean total consumption, temporally and spatially deflated, using national average prices as the base.

CHAPTER 6

An Empirical Model of Household Living Standards

Model Specification

In estimating model 1, consumption is expressed in real terms; that is, nominal consumption per capita is normalized by the spatial cost-of-living index that is implied by the region-specific poverty lines. This normalization is justifiable because the class of poverty measures used is homogeneous of degree zero in mean consumption and the poverty line; that is, the poverty measures $P_{\alpha j}$ only depend on the ratio of c_j to z. Thus, instead of evaluating poverty measures in terms of nominal consumption per capita using nominal poverty lines for different regions, we can evaluate them equivalently in terms of real consumption per capita using a single poverty line expressed in the same real units.

In the econometric analysis, we allow for regional heterogeneity by estimating separate models for five regions: three for rural areas and two for urban areas. The rural sample is split into three regions: northern (Niassa, Cabo Delgado, and Nampula provinces), central (Tete, Manica, Zambézia, and Sofala provinces), and southern (Gaza, Inhambane, and Maputo provinces). The urban areas are divided into large cities (Maputo, Matola, Beira, and Nampula), and all other areas are classified as urban in the IAF sample. We later test whether it is tenable to assume that there is no regional heterogeneity within urban and rural sectors.

Selection of Explanatory Variables

The set of variables that are hypothesized to determine consumption, and hence poverty, includes household and community characteristics. A key consideration in selecting from potential determinants of consumption is to choose variables that are arguably exogenous to current consumption. Thus, for instance, we do not include value or possession of durable goods in the set of explanatory variables because the imputed use value of durable goods is a component of consumption (see Appendix 1). Similarly, we do not include dwelling characteristics, as these are likely to be determined by household living standards; these characteristics determine actual or imputed rents that are also components of aggregate consumption for the household.

Also, variables such as current school attendance by children are deliberately omitted from the model, as they are arguably an outcome, rather than a determinant of current living standards. For such attributes, causality runs in the other direction. Our selection of potential determinants is also guided by the results of the poverty profile, which suggested some significant correlates of poverty in Mozambique, albeit based on bivariate associations (see

MPF/UEM/IFPRI 1998). This section describes the process for selecting variables for the empirical model, under the categories of demography, education, employment, agriculture, community characteristics, and access to services. Although efforts have been made to avoid endogenous variables as regressors, in some cases the exogeneity of selected variables is debatable. Finding suitable instruments for these variables is extremely difficult. For these cases, we test for endogeneity and test an alternative instrumental variables fixed-effects (IVFE) model.

Demographic Characteristics

The demographic data used include household size and composition variables. Four age categories are distinguished: under 10 years of age, 10–17, 18–59, and 60 years of age and above. The number of productive-age adults—the 18–59-year-old age group—is further split by gender.[29] We introduce a quadratic term in household size to allow for nonlinearities in the relationship between household size and living standards. The age and sex of the household head are also included in the model. Other things being equal, we expect households with a higher ratio of adults to children to have higher living standards. Based on experience in numerous other countries (Lanjouw and Ravallion 1995; Deaton and Paxson 1998), we expect a negative relationship between total household size and total consumption per capita, or total consumption per AEU.

Other household characteristics under the demographic category include a variable for the number of women in the household who had their first child before the age of 16 years, to capture the potential adverse effects of adolescent childbearing on household living standards (becoming a mother during adolescence may adversely affect a woman's schooling, labor force participation, or productivity).[30] The number of adult members with any physical or mental disability is also included. Finally, the number of members who are refugees or displaced because of the war is included as an explanatory variable. It is expected that each of these last two variables is negatively related to household living standards.

Education

We include several measures pertaining to different levels and dimensions of educational attainment in the household, based on the hypothesis that human capital (as measured by literacy and formal education) contributes positively to higher living standards. First, we include measures of the number of adult (18 years or older) household members who stated that they could read and write. We then include the number of adult members with full primary education (known as EP2, for *escola primária de 2° grau*) or higher.[31] As there is good reason to suppose that the returns to male and female education may be significantly different,[32] these variables are also differentiated by gender. We also include a variable that measures the maximum level of education attained by any household member to see if this has an independent effect, as has been demonstrated in other research in Sub-Saharan Africa (Jolliffe 2002).

[29]We also include the number of household members with missing age as a separate variable. This variable, together with the other five household composition variables, sums exactly to the total household size.

[30]This characteristic is found to be strongly associated with poverty levels in the poverty profile (see MPF/UEM/IFPRI, Chapter 2).

[31]We experimented with the number of members, by gender, with postprimary education as separate variables, but abandoned this because extremely few women have postprimary education, especially in the rural north.

[32]There is evidence that points to the existence of gender differentials in the returns to education for other countries. For a review of the literature, see Schultz 1988.

Employment

In this category, we include variables relating to the distribution of occupations within households. In particular, three broad sectors of employment are distinguished: agriculture, including livestock and fisheries; industry, mining, and construction; and commerce, transport, communication, and other services. Three corresponding variables then give the total number of adults in the household employed in each sector. We also include a variable that measures diversification of income sources within the household, with a view to examining the hypothesis that multiple income sources contribute to lower risks and higher income for the household. This variable is specified as a count of the distinct number of income sources for the household and takes values up to four. As the exogeneity of the employment and income diversification variables is debatable, we conduct Hausman tests to examine this formally.

Agriculture, Land, and Livestock

The total area of the landholding (*machamba*) is included as a determinant of living standards, with the hypothesis that other things being equal, households with larger landholdings per capita will have higher living standards. In the IAF, landholding size was not measured, but was estimated by the respondents.[33] As the relationship between landholding and welfare in the data appears to be nonlinear, the square root of the area in hectares is used in the estimations; a log transformation is ruled out because of the presence of households with zero hectares. We also include a dummy variable to indicate if the household has irrigated land or used inputs such as fertilizers, pesticides, plows, motor pumps, or fumigation equipment. Because these inputs are potentially endogenous, we conduct Hausman tests for them as well.[34] We define a variable to indicate the type and relative security of land tenure. In the model, land tenure is considered relatively insecure if land was acquired through informal occupation, on a rental basis, or borrowed.

Households are also distinguished by the type of crops they cultivate; three binary variables are included to indicate the cultivation of basic food crops, horticultural crops, and commercial crops.[35] Similarly, variables are also included for the number

[33]We also considered cultivated area, as opposed to cultivable area, but the two variables were highly correlated (correlation coefficient of 0.93) as households tended to cultivate all the land they had. Of the two, total landholding is preferred, largely because the area cultivated variable is only reported as a proportion of the reported landholdings, with only four coding options: less than half, half, more than half, and all. Furthermore, endogeneity is less of a problem with the landholding variable than it is with the area cultivated variable, as area cultivated is always determined in the current crop year, whereas landholding is typically determined by land clearing decisions made in previous years.

[34]As with employment and income diversification, it would be preferable to use instrumental variables for these potentially endogenous variables. However, it was not possible to identify suitable instruments for these specific variables. As an alternative, an instrumental variables-fixed-effects (IVFE) estimator was considered, which is reported later in this section.

[35]For these variables we follow the classification used by the IAF survey protocol (Cavero 1998). Basic food crops are maize, cassava, sorghum, millet, rice, groundnuts, potatoes, sweet potatoes, beans, and sesame. Horticultural crops are onions, tomatoes, all leafy green vegetables, pumpkins, peas, okra, carrots, yams, melons, peppers, garlic, eggplant, and cucumber. Commercial crops are defined as cotton, coffee, sugarcane, tea, ginger, sunflower, sisal, soybeans, and tobacco.

of cashew, citrus, or coconut trees,[36] and other fruit trees that a household has.

Two variables to indicate the household's possession of livestock are employed. The first measures the number of cattle, sheep, goats, pigs, and rabbits that the household owns, which are combined using a set of tropical livestock units (TLU), as described in ILCA (1990). The ILCA TLU scale does not include values for swine and rabbits, so estimated TLU values of 0.2 and 0.005 are used here.[37] The second livestock variable is a simple count of the number of chickens and other fowl owned by the household. Both the crop choice and livestock ownership variables are potentially endogenous, and we test for endogeneity of these variables.

Community Characteristics and Access to Services

From the community module of the IAF, a number of potential variables are available to reflect rural households' access to infrastructure and services. For instance, there are variables to indicate if the village where the household resides has a bank, a market, an agriculture and livestock extension center, a post office, a public telephone, or if a paved or dirt road passes through that village.[38] Similarly, there are also variables to indicate the presence of health services in the village, including a doctor, nurse, midwife, health center, health post, or traditional healer. We initially tried to identify the separate effects of individual community facilities; however, with our data, these individual effects were estimated imprecisely. Therefore, these variables are aggregated into two indexes of infrastructure development. The first is an economic infrastructure index, which is the simple average of six binary variables indicating the presence of the following six individual facilities in the village: bank, market, agriculture and livestock extension center, post office, public telephone, and paved or improved dirt road. The second is an index of health infrastructure, which is the simple average of four binary variables representing the presence in the village of a doctor, nurse, health center, or sanitary post.

To capture the effects of additional health factors, a dummy variable to indicate if malaria is reported to be the principal health problem in a community is also included.

Seasonal Effects

It is well established that in predominantly agrarian societies such as Mozambique, there is a strong seasonal variation in welfare levels, which is related to the agricultural calendar. The IAF survey design accommodates these fluctuations in part by spreading household interviews over the entire year. If interviews were conducted only in the relatively rich postharvest period, living standards would appear to be better and poverty levels lower than they really are. The opposite would hold if interviews were only conducted in the preharvest period, when food and cash are extremely scarce. However, spreading the survey out only avoids (or reduces) the problem of measuring in different seasons for aggregate measures such as mean consumption or average poverty levels. It does not avoid the problem of a household's measured welfare level being dependent on

[36]Coconut is included in the same variable as citrus because of its economic importance in the coastal zones of Zambézia and Inhambane provinces. All other fruit trees are included in the "other" category.

[37]For comparison, the TLU values for cattle, sheep, and goats are 0.7, 0.1, and 0.1, respectively.

[38]The community questionnaire from which these variables are derived also provides the distances from the village to these services, but we consider this information unreliable and, hence, limit our specification to binary variables indicating the presence of such services in the village.

the season of the interview. For example, consider two identical households, one (household A) interviewed in July (postharvest) and the other (household B) interviewed in January (preharvest). The measure of consumption (welfare) would indicate that household A is richer than household B, but a reversal of interview dates would also reverse the ranking. In this analysis, we control for seasonal effects by incorporating a set of monthly dummy variables.

Definition of the Dependent Variable

As discussed earlier, the welfare measure used in this study is total consumption per capita, with the nominal consumption measure adjusted for the cost of acquiring a region-specific basic needs bundle in each of the 13 poverty line regions. Although consumption is widely accepted as a measure of poverty—specifically income poverty—there are subtleties in the scaling or normalization of the measure that may affect welfare comparisons. We address the two most critical here. One is the practice of using consumption per capita versus consumption per AEU. The other is the choice of using a single national basic needs food bundle versus multiple, region-specific food bundles in the creation of the food poverty line, and hence, the mapping of consumption from nominal terms to real terms.

The principal argument for using an AEU scale is that consumption requirements for some individuals, most notably children, are significantly lower than those for adults. This is clear if the consumption item in question is food energy, although it is less clear for other consumption items, such as health care or education. If, on balance, consumption requirements differ by age and sex categories, a per capita measure will misclassify living standards at the individual and household levels.[39] Consider two five-person households, with equal levels of consumption per capita in monetary terms. One has five adult males and the other has an adult female and four young children. Food energy requirements will be higher in the household of adult males, and if food is a large share of the total consumption bundle, total consumption requirements will be higher in that household as well. A given level of consumption per capita will be insufficient to meet the needs of the adult male household but will be adequate for the other household. Use of an appropriate AEU scale avoids such misclassification. We first estimate model 1 with consumption per capita as the dependent variable; we then reestimate it with consumption per AEU on the left-hand side, defining the poverty lines in AEU terms as well. We adopt an AEU scale that is based upon the age- and sex-specific caloric requirements in Table 4.2.

The other factor that may affect welfare comparisons pertains to the definition of the reference food bundle for the food poverty line, which, on average, makes up about three-quarters of the total poverty line. As discussed in Chapter 4, most poverty analyses using the cost-of-basic-needs approach specify a single food bundle for all regions of the country, so that any interregional differences in the level of food poverty lines arise entirely from interregional differences in prices of foods in the bundle. As there is evidence of considerable substitution in basic foods across regions in Mozambique, because of large differences in relative prices (Tarp et al. 2002b), we choose to

[39]Although this classification may easily occur at the household level, Eastwood and Lipton (1999), among others, have observed that consumption per AEU seldom ranks large groups differently from consumption per capita.

allow the food bundle to vary by region. While we believe that this choice is justifiable on theoretical and empirical grounds, it is also advisable to undertake sensitivity analysis to understand what, if any, impact this decision has on the results of this study.

We examine the sensitivity of the results to these choices by estimating the consumption model with three different specifications of the dependent variable. The first specification, which we prefer for reasons elaborated earlier, is to estimate real consumption per capita, with the conversion from nominal to real meticais determined by a set of poverty lines based on region-specific food bundles. The second is to estimate real consumption per AEU, again using the poverty lines based on region-specific food consumption bundles. The third specification estimates consumption per capita, but converts nominal to real values using poverty lines based on a single national food consumption bundle (see Tarp et al. 2002b for additional details).

Model Estimation

The first estimation issue has to do with missing values in the data set for a number of explanatory variables. Even though the number of missing observations for any single variable is not large, the set of households for whom there is missing data for at least one variable increases with the number of explanatory variables. As we are using a large set of variables to predict consumption, we opt to include observations with missing data by constructing a set of dummy variables that take the value of one if the household is missing data for a particular variable, and zero otherwise; missing values of the variable in question are set to zero. This way we reduce the potential of sample selection bias, and we do not exclude useful information from households that have valid data for most explanatory variables.

As noted above, there are also some concerns of potential bias in parameter estimates because of omitted variables or endogenous explanatory variables. For instance, it could be argued that agroecological factors that determine the productivity of land are omitted from the regression and are therefore included implicitly in the error term of the model. If these factors are a significant determinant of living standards, the error term will not converge to zero in probability limit, and the parameter estimates for the included explanatory variables will be inconsistent.

Another variant of this problem could be described by the argument that the effect of some of the determinants, for instance, whether there is a market in the village or whether a household cultivates horticultural or commercial crops, themselves depend on the omitted agroecological factors. Because the omitted factors are subsumed by the error term, these determinants would now be correlated with the error term, and hence give rise to inconsistent parameter estimates.

One approach for dealing with the potential problem of omitted variables is the use of a fixed-effects model. For instance, a set of village dummy variables will control for all observed and unobserved village-level determinants of living standards. For our data and model, we decided to introduce fixed effects at the district level, where each district contains several sample communities. As we want to analyze community-level variables (in the rural model, where community-level data are available), we cannot introduce fixed effects at the village level, because the village-level fixed-effects estimator will absorb all community-level information and preclude the analysis of the specific effects of any particular community variable. There are 112 districts covered in the rural sample, 20 in the urban sample, and we argue that including district-level fixed effects controls for much of the potential omitted variable bias.

A potential limitation of a model along the lines of equation (1) is that the marginal effect of a determinant on log per capita consumption is the same across all households within the domain of estimation. However, it could be argued that the marginal effect of a variable depends on other household characteristics. For instance, the marginal effect of a bank or market in the village itself could depend upon the education levels of household members. This suggests a generalization of model 1, where some determinants of living standards are interacted with each other (for an example of such an approach, see Datt and Jolliffe 1999).

However, such an augmentation of the model comes at a price. The interaction terms can be highly collinear with other variables in the model. This can often lead to highly imprecise—and volatile—parameter estimates, which can in turn produce misleading results in simulations where only a select subset of variables are altered at a time. Thus, we opt to introduce only a limited set of interaction terms. For the urban model, these are limited to the interaction of male and female literacy variables with the sector of employment. For the rural model, in addition to these, we also include interactions of the literacy variables with the community-level indexes of infrastructure development. These particular interactions are chosen because the components can be hypothesized to have synergistic effects. For example, while the presence of services in a community may enhance well-being, it might be expected that the effect is greater among those who are better placed to take advantage of the service (for example, the better educated members of the community). Likewise, service- and commercial-sector employment in urban areas covers a wide range of occupations, from cleaning staff and domestic servants to professionals. Interacting sector of employment with literacy helps discriminate between these occupations.

Thus, our initial specification is model 1 with district fixed effects and limited interaction among the x_j determinants. This model is estimated separately for rural and urban sectors, with the rural model including community-level variables that were not collected in urban areas. For the rural model, the parameters are allowed to vary for the northern, central, and southern regions. The parameters for the urban model are also allowed to differ for two classifications of urban areas: the four large cities and other urban areas. To permit the parameters to vary by geographic area, and facilitate hypothesis testing for the equality of parameters across regions (or urban classification), we estimate the rural model by interacting the explanatory variables with dummy variables for each of the three regions. An analogous procedure is followed for the two categories of urban areas. This approach also accommodates the few instances in which we choose not to allow a parameter to vary by region, because the explanatory variable has extremely limited variation within one or more regions. For instance, there are only 14 of 1,905 households in the total rural north sample that had an adult female with full primary or higher level of education (EP2 or above). For the rural areas as a whole, only 1.5 percent of the sample households have an adult female with primary or higher education. For variables such as this, it is not possible to identify precise region-specific effects; in these cases, our preferred estimates allow for only a single, region-invariant effect.[40]

Summary statistics for all of the variables in the rural and urban models can be found in Tables 6.1 and 6.2, respectively.

[40]The variables controlling for missing data for particular explanatory variables also are not interacted with regional dummy variables.

Table 6.1 Means and standard errors of variables in rural determinants of poverty model

Variable	Northern	Central	Southern	All rural
N	1,905	2,288	1,618	5,811
Ln of real consumption per person per day	8.573	8.376	8.384	8.451
	(0.031)	(0.031)	(0.039)	(0.019)
Persons 0–9 years old	1.411	1.555	1.530	1.498
	(0.052)	(0.040)	(0.047)	(0.028)
Persons 10–17 years old	0.738	1.026	1.153	0.941
	(0.035)	(0.040)	(0.043)	(0.023)
Females 18–59 years old	1.000	1.093	1.327	1.098
	(0.019)	(0.017)	(0.031)	(0.012)
Males 18–59 years old	0.877	0.908	0.812	0.880
	(0.019)	(0.016)	(0.031)	(0.012)
Persons 60 years or older	0.189	0.161	0.418	0.215
	(0.020)	(0.015)	(0.021)	(0.011)
Persons of unclassified age	0.000	0.001	0.001	0.001
	(0.000)	(0.000)	(0.001)	(0.000)
Household size squared	22.167	28.057	37.059	27.392
	(0.961)	(0.968)	(1.548)	(0.631)
Age of head of household	41.201	40.937	48.696	42.340
	(0.680)	(0.687)	(0.581)	(0.445)
Male head of household? (no=0; yes=1)	0.853	0.767	0.695	0.787
	(0.016)	(0.019)	(0.015)	(0.011)
Number of disabled persons in household	0.096	0.090	0.107	0.095
	(0.008)	(0.008)	(0.009)	(0.005)
Number of war migrants in household	0.066	0.275	0.150	0.177
	(0.019)	(0.052)	(0.072)	(0.028)
Number of women who had first child before age 16	0.236	0.113	0.057	0.149
	(0.013)	(0.008)	(0.006)	(0.006)
Number of literate adult males	0.454	0.517	0.589	0.506
	(0.023)	(0.025)	(0.031)	(0.015)
Number of literate adult females	0.095	0.157	0.421	0.179
	(0.019)	(0.018)	(0.028)	(0.012)
Number of adult males who completed primary education	0.039	0.046	0.054	0.045
	(0.006)	(0.007)	(0.007)	(0.004)
Number of adult females who completed primary education	0.007	0.006	0.027	0.010
	(0.002)	(0.002)	(0.004)	(0.001)
Highest level of education completed	1.360	1.321	1.607	1.383
	(0.064)	(0.066)	(0.065)	(0.041)
Number of adults in agricultural sector	1.782	1.890	2.070	1.880
	(0.038)	(0.035)	(0.060)	(0.023)
Number of adults in industrial or construction sectors	0.037	0.034	0.109	0.048
	(0.009)	(0.006)	(0.013)	(0.005)
Number of adults employed in other sectors	0.059	0.057	0.090	0.063
	(0.010)	(0.008)	(0.012)	(0.005)
Number of income sources	1.216	1.813	1.113	1.475
	(0.027)	(0.080)	(0.013)	(0.046)
Interaction: Male literacy x employed in industrial/construction sector	0.027	...	...	...
	(0.008)			
Interaction: Female literacy x employed in agricultural sector	...	...	1.100	...
			(0.082)	

(continued)

Table 6.1—Continued

Variable	Northern	Central	Southern	All rural
Square root of arable land (hectares)	1.303	1.180	1.648	1.304
	(0.030)	(0.024)	(0.044)	(0.018)
Use any equipment or irrigation? (no=0; yes=1)	0.062	0.024	0.113	0.053
	(0.018)	(0.005)	(0.020)	(0.008)
Secure land tenure? (no=0; yes=1)	0.332	0.498	0.716	0.473
	(0.020)	(0.024)	(0.022)	(0.014)
Cultivate horticultural crops? (no=0; yes=1)	0.072	0.269	0.426	0.223
	(0.018)	(0.041)	(0.033)	(0.022)
Cultivate commercial crops? (no=0; yes=1)	0.120	0.044	0.011	0.067
	(0.034)	(0.014)	(0.004)	(0.014)
Ln of number of cashew trees	0.490	0.420	1.588	0.642
	(0.096)	(0.069)	(0.150)	(0.057)
Ln of number of citrus trees plus coconut trees	0.255	0.424	1.132	0.481
	(0.069)	(0.073)	(0.156)	(0.050)
Ln of number of other trees	0.417	0.826	1.367	0.766
	(0.037)	(0.051)	(0.106)	(0.036)
Tropical livestock units (cattle, sheep, goats)	0.118	0.242	0.434	0.229
	(0.022)	(0.061)	(0.044)	(0.030)
Number of poultry	4.141	6.898	7.736	6.019
	(0.369)	(0.792)	(0.641)	(0.427)
Economic infrastructure index	0.163	0.113	0.171	0.141
	(0.017)	(0.012)	(0.025)	(0.009)
Interaction: Economic infrastructure index x Adult female literacy	0.018	0.019	0.086	0.030
	(0.004)	(0.003)	(0.018)	(0.003)
Health infrastructure index	0.108	0.065	0.187	0.101
	(0.017)	(0.011)	(0.028)	(0.009)
Malaria identified as the major health problem? (no=0; yes=1)	0.385	0.382	0.664	0.430
	(0.049)	(0.052)	(0.047)	(0.032)

Source: Mozambique National Household Survey of Living Conditions, 1996–97.
Note: Standard errors are in parentheses, corrected for sample design effects.

Endogeneity Issues

As noted earlier, several of the explanatory variables considered in the empirical model of per capita consumption are arguably endogenous. The most questionable variables are the sector of employment, the number of income sources, and several of the agriculture variables (production of certain types of crops, livestock ownership, landholdings, and the use of irrigation or improved inputs). Ideally, one would use an instrumented variables approach to replace these variables with exogenous regressors. However, we were unable to identify instruments for these variables. We therefore adopted two different approaches to the question of endogenous regressors. The first is a set of Hausman tests for the exogeneity of the regressors and the second is a test of a specific form of instrumental variables estimator, in which the district fixed effects are used as instruments.

The general Hausman specification test can be used to test whether there exist systematic differences in two estimators: one that is consistent and one that is efficient under the assumption being tested (Hausman 1978; Greene 1997). The null hypothesis is that the efficient estimator is also consistent, in which case there should be no systematic differences in the parameter estimates of the two estimators. In the context of testing for endogeneity, the model with the suspected endogenous variable is the ef-

Table 6.2 Means and standard errors of variables in urban determinants of poverty model

Variable	Large cities	Small urban areas	All urban
N	1,570	869	2,439
Ln of real consumption per person per day	8.574	8.487	8.539
	(0.082)	(0.080)	(0.050)
Persons 0–9 years old	1.687	1.722	1.701
	(0.040)	(0.054)	(0.032)
Persons 10–17 years old	1.361	1.097	1.255
	(0.036)	(0.138)	(0.066)
Females 18–59 years old	1.243	1.031	1.158
	(0.037)	(0.047)	(0.028)
Males 18–59 years old	1.218	0.972	1.119
	(0.038)	(0.068)	(0.038)
Persons 60 years or older	0.163	0.221	0.187
	(0.020)	(0.031)	(0.021)
Persons of unclassified age	0.000	0.007	0.003
	(0.000)	(0.005)	(0.002)
Household size squared	40.423	32.891	37.393
	(1.486)	(2.885)	(1.457)
Age of head of household	41.706	41.176	41.493
	(0.637)	(0.785)	(0.501)
Male head of household? (no=0; yes=1)	0.790	0.758	0.777
	(0.012)	(0.022)	(0.011)
Number of disabled persons in household	0.071	0.101	0.083
	(0.008)	(0.016)	(0.008)
Number of war migrants in household	0.135	0.024	0.091
	(0.034)	(0.014)	(0.022)
Number of women who had first child before age 16	0.100	0.126	0.110
	(0.019)	(0.017)	(0.011)
Number of literate adult males	1.169	0.785	1.014
	(0.046)	(0.100)	(0.055)
Number of literate adult females	0.873	0.460	0.707
	(0.053)	(0.068)	(0.041)
Number of adult males who completed primary education	0.413	0.286	0.362
	(0.036)	(0.062)	(0.033)
Number of adult females who completed primary education	0.229	0.098	0.176
	(0.027)	(0.026)	(0.019)
Highest educational level of any adult in the household	3.122	2.328	2.803
	(0.083)	(0.297)	(0.150)
Number of adults in agricultural sector	0.417	0.930	0.623
	(0.069)	(0.122)	(0.072)
Number of adults in industrial or construction sectors	0.298	0.168	0.245
	(0.033)	(0.017)	(0.021)
Number of adults in other sectors	0.780	0.396	0.626
	(0.054)	(0.082)	(0.045)
Number of income sources	1.226	1.226	1.226
	(0.029)	(0.063)	(0.026)
Interaction: female literacy x employment in "other" sector	0.912	. . .	. . .
	(0.093)		
Interaction: male literacy x employment in agricultural sector	. . .	0.640	. . .
		(0.090)	

(continued)

Table 6.2—Continued

Variable	Large cities	Small urban areas	All urban
Interaction: female literacy x employment in agricultural sector	. . .	0.371	. . .
	(0.062)		
Interaction: female literacy x employment in industrial/construction sector	. . .	0.087	. . .
		(0.017)	
Square root of arable land (hectares)	0.486	0.804	0.614
	(0.062)	(0.064)	(0.039)
Use any equipment or irrigation? (no=0; yes=1)	0.061	0.092	0.074
	(0.010)	(0.020)	(0.009)
Secure land tenure? (no=0; yes=1)	0.213	0.401	0.289
	(0.024)	(0.036)	(0.018)
Ln of total number of fruit and nut trees	0.333	0.805	0.523
	(0.073)	(0.093)	(0.057)
Tropical livestock units (cattle, sheep, goats)	0.026	0.149	0.076
	(0.008)	(0.045)	(0.0174)
Number of poultry	1.456	2.117	1.722
	(0.397)	(0.373)	(0.263)

Source: Mozambique National Household Survey of Living Conditions, 1996–97.
Note: Standard errors are in parentheses, corrected for sample design effects.

ficient estimator, and a similar model that omits the suspected endogenous variable is the consistent estimator. Hausman specification tests for each of the possibly endogenous variables noted above are unable to reject the null hypothesis, so there is no evidence that the inclusion of these variables affects the estimates of other parameters in the model.

In addition to these Hausman tests, we also consider the alternative of the instrumental variables fixed-effects (IVFE) estimator. In the IVFE model, the fixed effects are used as instruments for all of the explanatory variables. The standard fixed-effects model is also known as the "within" estimator, because the coefficients are determined entirely by variation within the fixed-effects category; in our case, it means that the coefficients are based on variation within districts. The IVFE, on the other hand, is the "between" estimator, in that coefficients are estimated from the variation between district level means. These differences are highlighted in equations (5) and (6), which show the within and between estimators, respectively:

$$\beta^{within} : \ln c_{dj} = \beta' x_{dj} + \alpha_d + \varepsilon_{dj} \quad (5)$$

$$\beta^{between} : \overline{\ln c_d} = \beta' \bar{x}_d + \bar{\alpha}_d + \bar{\varepsilon}_d \quad (6)$$

The appropriateness of the IVFE model can be assessed by the same Hausman specification test, but this time in the context of testing fixed-effects versus random-effects specifications. The random effects model is a matrix-weighted average of the within and between estimators, so that rejection of the random effects model also implies rejection of the IVFE model. For the rural model, the random effects specification is soundly rejected (χ^2 = 401.75 (104), $p < 0.0000$).

Although the Hausman test cannot reject the random effects specification for the urban model, we opt to retain the fixed-effects specification because of the large efficiency loss associated with the IVFE specification. As the IVFE is based on district-level means, the effective size of the sample is reduced by a factor of 50, leaving few degrees of freedom.

Sensitivity with respect to Dependent Variable Specification

At the level of the model estimation, varying the dependent variable provides little information about the sensitivity of the results to these specification choices. For the AEU specification, it is not surprising that all of the parameter estimates are different than the model with per capita normalization, because the dependent variable is completely rescaled. Because most households have at least one child and at least one woman, all of the households in the survey have more persons in the household than they do adult equivalent units. The monetary value of consumption per AEU is therefore correspondingly higher than consumption per capita because the same numerator is being divided by a smaller denominator. What is relevant for the sensitivity analysis is how this rescaling varies across households.

The comparison of the regression results between the models using region-specific food bundles and a single national food bundle is even less informative. The poverty line method enters the analysis in the conversion of nominal consumption as captured by the survey to real consumption, in which the purchasing power of a unit of currency is made equal in each region. Because none of the 13 poverty line regions defined in Chapter 4 cross district boundaries, the coefficients for the district fixed effects absorb all of the differences in the dependent variable that arise from the poverty line method, leaving all of the other parameters unchanged.

The sensitivity of the results to the definition of the dependent variable can be assessed better in the context of the poverty reduction simulations presented in Chapter 8, where we will return to this subject.

CHAPTER 7

Estimation Results

Preferred Estimates

We subject the initial model estimates to a limited pruning, deleting interaction terms for coefficients that are not significant at the 10 percent level. These terms are deleted conditional on the acceptance of a Wald test for their joint deletion.[41] We also test for the joint significance of district fixed effects. The null hypothesis of the joint insignificance of district fixed effects (that is, that each of the coefficients for the district dummy variables is not significantly different from zero) is convincingly rejected for both rural and urban models (Tables 7.1 and 7.2). The fixed-effects specification is therefore retained in our preferred models.

We investigate the possibility of regional heterogeneity in the effects of different determinants on living standards. Thus, for the rural model, we test for equality of parameter estimates across the northern, central, and southern regions and find that this homogeneity hypothesis is strongly rejected (Table 7.1). Similarly, for the urban model, there is no support for the hypothesis of identical parameter estimates for the large city and other urban areas, so separate sets of coefficients for large and small urban areas are retained (Table 7.2).

The preferred parameter estimates are also subjected to collinearity diagnostics. The variance inflation factors for the parameters do not indicate this to be a serious concern.[42] Diagnostic tests for influential observations using *dfbeta* statistics (see Belsley, Kuh, and Welsch 1980) also confirm that the parameter estimates are not unduly influenced by a small subset of observations. A detailed discussion of the regression results follows, beginning with the rural model.

Rural Determinants of Consumption and Poverty

Table 7.1 presents the parameter estimates and standard errors for the rural model, with the parameter estimates for each of the three regions. The fit of the fixed-effects model is good, with

---

[41]In these and subsequent tests, we use a variance matrix corrected for sample design effects, allowing for both the stratified and clustered nature of our sample. We use the routines for robust variance estimation in the software package *Stata* (Stata Corp. 2003), which use the Huber/White sandwich estimator described by Rogers (1993) and Williams (2000).

[42]The highest variance inflation factors for the rural and urban models were 20.95 and 19.05, respectively (with the exception of binary variables for the central and northern regions in the rural model and the monthly dummy variables).

Table 7.1 Determinants of rural poverty in Mozambique

Variable	Northern	Central	Southern
Intercept	9.815	...	...
	(0.164)		
Central region	...	0.822	...
		(0.174)	
Demographic variables			
Age of household head	–0.000	–0.001	–0.002
	(0.001)	(0.001)	(0.001)
Male head of household	0.141	0.083	0.033
	(0.038)	(0.032)	(0.029)
Number of members 0–9 years old	–0.399	–0.356	–0.296
	(0.027)	(0.017)	(0.030)
Number of members 10–17 years old	–0.355	–0.321	–0.281
	(0.026)	(0.016)	(0.027)
Number of women 18–59 years old	–0.447	–0.425	–0.308
	(0.042)	(0.034)	(0.040)
Number of men 18–59 years old	–0.434	–0.383	–0.322
	(0.047)	(0.030)	(0.043)
Number of members 60 years old or older	–0.463	–0.407	–0.356
	(0.049)	(0.038)	(0.040)
Number of persons of unclassified age	–0.411	–0.356	0.337
	(0.070)	(0.255)	(0.465)
Household size squared	0.020	0.015	0.012
	(0.002)	(0.001)	(0.002)
Number of persons with disabilities	–0.018	0.005	–0.086
	(0.039)	(0.031)	(0.034)
Number of war migrants	–0.002	–0.034	0.007
	(0.016)	(0.017)	(0.017)
Number of females who had first child before age 16	–0.058	0.060	–0.002
	(0.028)	(0.033)	(0.059)
Education variables			
Number of adult males who can read and write	0.036	0.033	0.057
	(0.026)	(0.022)	(0.026)
Number of adult females who can read and write	–0.045	0.074	0.186
	(0.049)	(0.028)	(0.047)
Number of adult males who completed primary school	0.026	0.026	0.026
	(0.032)	(0.032)	(0.032)
Number of adult females who completed primary school	0.088	0.088	0.088
	(0.058)	(0.058)	(0.058)
Highest educational level of any adult household member	0.049	0.054	0.042
	(0.016)	(0.013)	(0.0162)
Employment variables			
Number of adults employed in agriculture	0.043	0.040	0.046
	(0.030)	(0.024)	(0.022)
Number of adults employed in industry or construction	0.189	0.051	0.127
	(0.102)	(0.054)	(0.050)
Number of adults employed in other sectors	0.353	0.272	0.118
	(0.052)	(0.053)	(0.047)
Number of sources of income	0.010	–0.030	0.087
	(0.031)	(0.028)	(0.039)
Agriculture variables			
Square root of land area	0.038	0.030	0.006
	(0.034)	(0.021)	(0.032)

(continued)

Table 7.1—Continued

Variable	Northern	Central	Southern
Secure land tenure	–0.048	0.006	–0.029
	(0.029)	(0.026)	(0.035)
Livestock ownership (tropical livestock units)	0.023	0.009	0.039
	(0.019)	(0.005)	(0.013)
Number of poultry owned	0.001	0.003	0.005
	(0.001)	(0.001)	(0.001)
Log of the number of cashew trees	0.016	0.006	0.003
	(0.013)	(0.018)	(0.010)
Log of the number of citrus trees	0.004	0.010	0.039
	(0.020)	(0.014)	(0.012)
Log of the number of other fruit or nut trees	0.012	0.027	0.039
	(0.012)	(0.011)	(0.011)
Household produces horticultural crops	–0.003	–0.002	–0.003
	(0.023)	(0.023)	(0.023)
Household produces commercial crops	0.034	0.034	0.034
	(0.036)	(0.036)	(0.036)
Household uses irrigation or other improved agricultural equipment	0.057	0.057	0.057
	(0.037)	(0.037)	(0.037)
Community variables			
Economic infrastructure index	0.146	0.146	0.146
	(0.096)	(0.098)	(0.096)
Economic infrastructure x Number of literate adult females	0.141	0.141	0.141
	(0.047)	(0.047)	(0.047)
Health infrastructure index	0.052	0.052	0.052
	(0.066)	(0.066)	(0.066)
Malaria cited as principal health problem in village	–0.018	–0.018	–0.018
	(0.034)	(0.034)	(0.034)
Selected interaction terms			
Male literacy x Number employed in industry or commerce	–0.089	...	...
	(0.107)		
Female literacy x Number employed in agriculture	...	...	–0.042
			(0.012)

Number of observations = 5,811
Number of primary sampling units = 196
Number of strata = 10
$R^2 = 0.5457$
Adjusted $R^2 = 0.5271$
Root mean squared error = 0.4845

Tests of hypotheses

Coefficients in Northern = coefficients in Central	F(25, 162) =	1.99	Prob > F =	0.0058
Coefficients in Northern = coefficients in Southern	F(26, 161) =	3.23	Prob > F =	0.0000
Coefficients in Central = coefficients in Southern	F(26, 161) =	2.02	Prob > F =	0.0045
Monthly dummies	F(14, 173) =	5.77	Prob > F =	0.0000
District fixed effects	F(110, 77) =	141.59	Prob > F =	0.0000

Notes: The F-statistic for the regression is $F(k, d-k+1)$, where k = number of estimated parameters, d = total number of sampled primary sampling units minus the total number of strata. The F-statistics for the tests of hypotheses are $F(r, d-r+1)$ where r = number of restrictions tested. The regression and the tests are implemented using Stata's svyreg and svytest commands. See Korn and Graubard (1990) for a detailed explanation of degrees of freedom (cited in Stata Reference Manual, Release 5, Volume 3).

Table 7.2 Determinants of urban poverty in Mozambique

Variable	Large urban areas	Small urban areas
Intercept	8.820	...
	(0.213)	
Demographic variables		
Age of household head	0.004	–0.001
	(0.002)	(0.001)
Male head of household	0.186	0.153
	(0.048)	(0.058)
Number of members 0–9 years old	–0.297	–0.365
	(0.020)	(0.028)
Number of members 10–17 years old	–0.240	–0.281
	(0.017)	(0.045)
Number of women 18–59 years old	–0.440	–0.433
	(0.033)	(0.077)
Number of men 18–59 years old	–0.368	–0.298
	(0.057)	(0.068)
Number of members 60 years old or older	–0.400	–0.312
	(0.053)	(0.066)
Number of persons of unclassified age	–0.341	–0.413
	(0.515)	(0.559)
Household size squared	0.010	0.015
	(0.001)	(0.002)
Number of persons with disabilities	0.014	–0.083
	(0.060)	(0.060)
Number of war migrants	0.002	–0.072
	(0.020)	(0.078)
Number of females who had first child before age 16	–0.095	–0.040
	(0.055)	(0.050)
Education variables		
Number of adult males who can read and write	0.027	0.067
	(0.056)	(0.057)
Number of adult females who can read and write	0.248	0.093
	(0.035)	(0.081)
Number of adult males who completed primary school	0.043	0.101
	(0.036)	(0.066)
Number of adult females who completed primary school	0.113	0.119
	(0.040)	(0.071)
Highest educational level of any adult household member	0.173	0.086
	(0.023)	(0.033)
Employment variables		
Number of adults employed in agriculture	–0.035	–0.014
	(0.044)	(0.064)
Number of adults employed in industry or construction	0.028	–0.008
	(0.032)	(0.050)
Number of adults employed in other sectors	0.147	0.163
	(0.037)	(0.040)
Number of sources of income	–0.006	0.003
	(0.031)	(0.056)
Agriculture variables		
Square root of land area	–0.001	0.055
	(0.046)	(0.038)

(continued)

Table 7.2—Continued

Variable	Large urban areas	Small urban areas
Secure land tenure	–0.013	–0.111
	(0.067)	(0.039)
Livestock ownership (Tropical livestock units)	0.172	0.039
	(0.035)	(0.014)
Number of poultry owned	0.001	0.010
	(0.000)	(0.003)
Log of total number of fruit and nut trees	–0.049	0.045
	(0.036)	(0.019)
Household uses irrigation or other improved agricultural equipment	0.113	0.113
	(0.065)	(0.065)
Selected interaction terms		
Female literacy x Number employed in "other" employment sector	–0.053	
	(0.014)	
Female literacy x Number employed in agriculture		0.066
		(0.044)
Female literacy x Number employed in industry or construction sectors		0.153
		(0.096)
Male literacy x Number employed in agriculture		–0.075
		(0.028)

Number of observations = 2,439
Number of primary sampling units = 77
Number of strata = 11
R^2 = 0.5116
Adjusted R^2 = 0.4907
Root mean squared error = 0.6225

Tests of hypotheses:		
Coefficients in large = coefficients in small	F(26, 41) = 3.56	Prob > F = 0.0001
Monthly dummies	F(13, 54) = 2.93	Prob > F = 0.0028
District fixed effects	F(19, 48) = 4.88	Prob > F = 0.0000

Notes: Large urban areas are Maputo City, Matola, Beira, and Nampula City. Small urban areas are provincial capitals and other areas defined as urban under the sampling frame of the Mozambique National Household Survey of Living Conditions, 1996–97.
Also see notes to Table 7.1.

an adjusted R^2 of 0.527. The statistical significance of various parameter estimates varies widely, both across variables within a region and across regions for individual variables. There are also many variables that have strongly significant coefficients across all three rural regions. With only a few exceptions, the signs on the parameters are as expected, and the relative magnitudes of the parameters are also reasonable. Note that as the dependent variable is in natural logarithm form, the estimated regression coefficients measure the percentage change in consumption per capita from a unit change in the continuous independent variables. When the explanatory variable is a dummy variable, the interpretation is slightly different: the percentage change in dependent variable from a unit change in the dummy variable is approximately $e^{\hat{\beta}}-1$ (Halvorsen and Palmquist 1980; Kennedy 1981). We now turn to a more in-depth discussion of the regression results, by category of explanatory variable, starting with the demographic variables.

Demographic Characteristics

Given the strong negative relationship between household size and per capita consumption already noted in earlier work (MPF/UEM/IFPRI 1998), it is not entirely surprising that the estimated parameters are negative and highly significant for the six variables measuring the number of people in the household, disaggregated by age and sex. However, it is surprising that the coefficients are more negative for adults in the household than they are for children, a result that is consistent in all three regions. That is, according to the regression estimates, other things being equal, an additional adult in the household will reduce consumption per capita more than an additional child in the household will. This is counterintuitive, especially in light of the descriptive information on poverty and dependency ratios presented in MPF/UEM/IFPRI 1998.

The estimated coefficient on the quadratic term for household size is positive and significant, suggesting a U-shaped relationship between household size and consumption per capita, with the bottom of the U-shape occurring at approximately 10 to 12 persons, varying slightly by region. This implies that, on average and other things being equal, at household sizes of less than 12 persons (which comprises 99 percent of the rural sample), the addition of another person to the household reduces per capita consumption but at a decreasing rate.

However, these results are contingent on the implicit assumption regarding economies of household size in consumption noted earlier. The use of per capita consumption as the welfare measure carries the assumption of no economies of household size. This is a strong, and likely erroneous, assumption, as there are some "publicly consumed" components of household consumption (such as housing) that do not need to increase proportionately with household size to maintain a constant standard of living (Deaton and Paxson 1998).

We explore the effects of economies of household size (h) by calculating a modified consumption/welfare (c) measure, (c_j / h_j^{θ}), where $\theta = 1.0$ gives the per capita case, and $1 - \theta$ gives a measure of economies of household size (Lanjouw and Ravallion 1995). We experiment with values of 0.0, 0.2, 0.4, 0.6, 0.8, and 1.0 for θ. The poverty headcount is then calculated for each household size category, where the poverty line is normalized so that it pertains to a household of average size; that is, a household of average size has the same poverty headcount for all values of θ. The results are presented in Figure 7.1.[43] The line corresponding to $\theta = 1.0$ shows the expected pattern: as household size increases, so does the poverty headcount. For the other polar case, $\theta = 0$ (that is, complete economies of scale, or "two [and three, and four, and so forth] can live as cheaply as one"), the poverty headcount declines as household size increases. The correlation between household size and poverty headcount almost disappears when $\theta = 0.4$, as indicated by the relatively flat line for that value.

As suggested by Lanjouw and Ravallion (1995), one can interpret this result as a "critical value," against which one can assess plausible values of the true, but unknown, θ in a given setting. In an economy such as Mozambique's, where the budget share of privately consumed goods is high (for example, 68 percent for food), the true θ is likely to be high, probably in the neigh-

[43]As few households (only 343) have more than 10 members, the calculations in the "10+" persons category include all households with 10 or more members.

Figure 7.1 Poverty and household size, under alternative assumptions about economies of household size

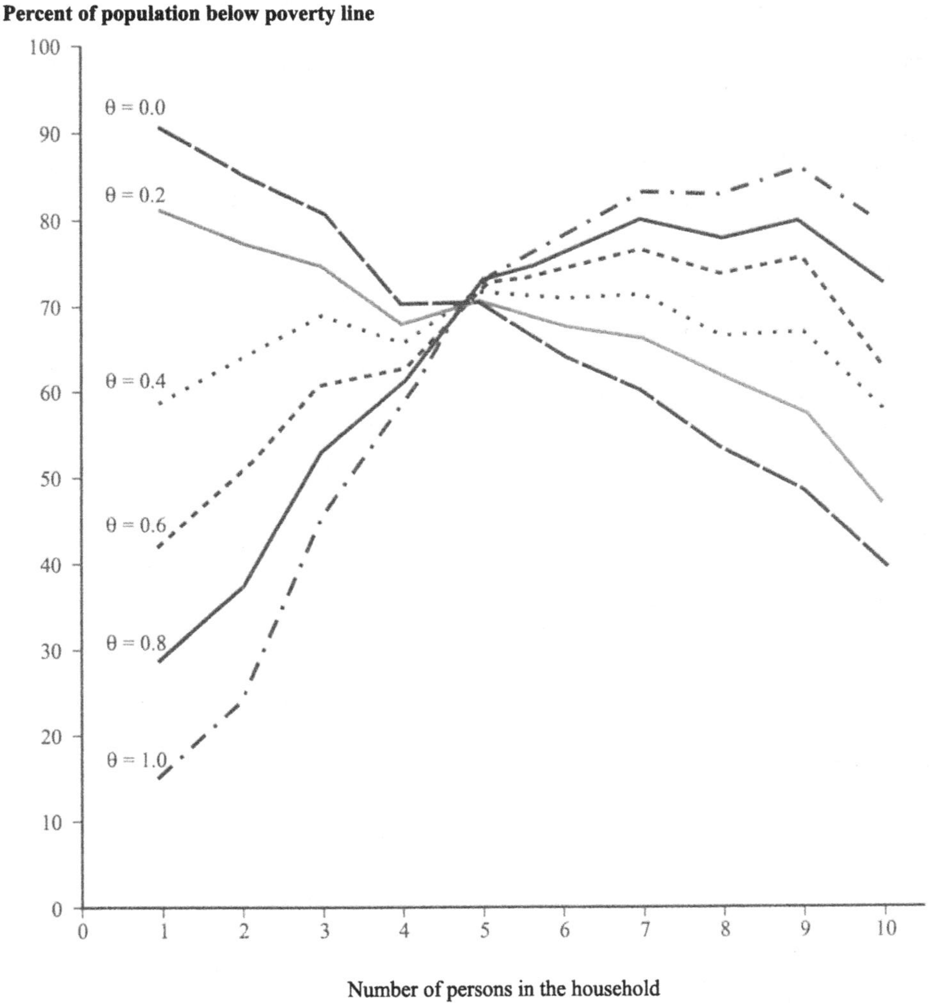

Source: Mozambique National Household Survey of Living Conditions, 1996–97

Notes: θ is a measure of the economies of scale of household size. When θ = 1 there are not economies of household size (that is, per capita normalization); when θ = 0 there are perfect economies of household size (that is, per household normalization).

borhood of 0.8 (Deaton 1997).[44] If this is the case, then the negative association observed between household size and welfare is not entirely an artifact of the per capita normalization. Rather, larger households are indeed poorer than smaller households, and the per capita normalization merely overstates the relationship somewhat.

To address the question of how sensitive the results are to the assumption of no

[44]Although even in the case of food, economies of household size can arise through practices such as bulk purchasing.

economies of household size that is implicit in the per capita measure, we also estimate the preferred model with consumption "per equivalent adult" (Lanjouw and Ravallion 1995). We use the size elasticity at which household size and poverty are almost orthogonal (0.6, corresponding to $\theta = 0.4$), and at a plausible estimate of the economies of household size in Mozambique (0.2, corresponding to $\theta = 0.8$). When the correlation between household size and poverty is eliminated ($\theta = 0.4$), the coefficients for the number of persons in the household become much smaller, ranging from –0.051 to only –0.152. Most of the other estimated parameters in the model do not change much in the alternative models. The principal exceptions are parameters for other demographic variables: those for age of household head become more negative and the squared term for household size remains positive, but the estimated coefficients are much smaller. When a plausible value is set for θ (0.8), the coefficients on household size are much closer to the per capita case, ranging from –0.204 to –0.358, with very little change in the other parameters.

The age of the household head does not have a significant effect on consumption per capita in any of the regions. However, the sex of the head of household does have a significant effect in the northern and central regions, with male-headed households having higher consumption per capita than female-headed households, all else being equal. The magnitude of the effect is 9 percent in the central region and 15 percent in the northern region.

This result appears to stand in contrast to the poverty profile, which notes that in rural areas, female-headed households are less likely to be poor than male-headed households, for all three poverty measures (MPF/UEM/IFPRI 1998).[45] Although it might appear that the regression results are inconsistent with the poverty profile, this is not the case. It is important to understand why and what the implications are for policy. The principal reason is that the regression analysis controls for the levels of other variables, whereas the poverty profile does not. Thus the regression analysis compares male- and female-headed households that have the same number of household members, the same amount of arable land, the same educational levels, and so forth. However, the average male- and female-headed households do not have the same values for these covariates. For example, rural female-headed households tend to be smaller than male-headed households (3.7 members versus 4.9 members, on average), and smaller households tend to be less poor. There are, no doubt, other variables that similarly confound the effect of the sex of the household head in the bivariate poverty profile analysis.

What does this contrast between the poverty profile and regression results imply for targeting female-headed households for poverty reduction efforts in Mozambique? The answer depends on the type of policy in question. If one is thinking of using female headship as a single targeting indicator for a transfer program directed to the poor, then the correct answer is given by the "unconditional" poverty profile, which suggests that female headship is not a good indicator of poverty. But, if, alternatively, the aim of policy intervention is to correct an underlying factor responsible for lower living standards, the factors identified by a multivari-

[45]The poverty profile reported in MPF/UEM/IFPRI (1998) also notes that, especially in the southern region, female-headed households are a heterogeneous group. De jure female heads (mostly widows and divorcees) tend to be poor, whereas de facto female heads (who are often married to men who have migrated to work in Maputo or South Africa) are less poor, on average, than male-headed households.

ate analysis provide the correct answer, although in this case female headship is not particularly amenable to policy interventions.[46]

The number of disabled persons in the household is only significant in the south, with the anticipated negative sign. The poverty profile results suggest an association between poverty and migration because of war (MPF/UEM/IFPRI 1998). In the regression analysis of the determinants of poverty, this effect is statistically significant only in the central region. The final demographic variable is the one for the number of women who are or were adolescent mothers (women currently between the ages of 12 and 49 who had their first child before the age of 16) in the household, which is also associated with higher poverty levels in the poverty profile. The regression coefficients for this variable are somewhat erratic, with the expected negative coefficient in the north (significant at the 5 percent level), a significant (at the 10 percent level) positive coefficient of the same magnitude in the center, and an insignificant effect in the south.

Education

Among the adult education variables, most have the expected positive association with consumption per capita, although several are not statistically significant. For adult literacy, the results are strongest in the south—both in terms of the magnitude of the coefficients and statistical significance—and diminish as one moves northward. Female literacy, in particular, has a large impact on consumption per capita: the coefficient for female literacy in the south is three times that of male literacy, and in the central region, the female coefficient is twice the size of the male literacy coefficient. The unexpected negative coefficient for female literacy in the north is not significantly different from zero, but even zero would be somewhat difficult to explain, given the number of studies that have shown the positive contributions of basic literacy.

Although both adult male and female primary education have the expected positive signs, neither is statistically significant at the 10 percent level. However, the variable for the maximum level of education of any adult household member is positive and significant in all three regions. This indicates that additional education for *at least* one member of the household has a positive effect on consumption per capita independent of the effect of the number of literate and primary school-educated household members. The significant positive effect of the maximum level of education also subsumes the effect of primary education. To confirm this, we reestimated the model, dropping the maximum education variable. On doing this, both the male and female primary education variables become significant at the 5 percent level or better.[47]

Employment and Income Sources

The three variables for number of adults employed in different economic sectors show the expected pattern. Most are statistically significant, and all are positive, indicating that, other things being equal, adult employment of any kind leads to higher

---

[46]There are examples of legislative attempts in this area in industrialized countries, such as recent efforts by the Bush administration in the United States to provide financial incentives for poor single mothers receiving federal assistance to get married. To our knowledge, there are no similar initiatives under consideration in Mozambique.

[47]The estimated parameter on male primary education is 0.092 with a *t*-ratio of 3.16, and that on female primary education is 0.133 with a *t*-ratio of 2.25.

consumption per capita than unemployment or unpaid housework.[48] The incremental gain in per capita consumption is smallest for those employed in agriculture and fisheries and largest for those employed in "other" sectors, a category that consists principally of services. The magnitude of some coefficients, particularly for other sectors, should be treated with some caution, as only a small proportion of the rural labor force is employed outside of agriculture, implying that the estimates for other sectors are based on relatively few observations. The variable for diversification of income sources is only statistically significant in the southern region, with the expected positive sign.

Agriculture and Livestock

Among the agriculture- and livestock-related variables, area of landholdings (with square root transformation) is not statistically significant in any of the regions. Recent studies by the Ministry of Agriculture and Fisheries and Michigan State University, using data collected from northern Mozambique, have argued that landholding size is an important determinant of per capita incomes (see, for example, de Marrule et al. 1998; Tschirley and Weber 1994; Mozambique, Ministry of Agriculture/MSU 1994). One possible explanation for this discrepancy is that in the IAF, land area was not measured but rather reported by sample households, who may only have a rough idea of the size of their land, particularly given the low level of input use. Thus, the IAF landholding data are relatively noisy, which reduces the ability to detect them as a determinant of consumption per capita.

The use of some equipment or irrigation, production of crops that are strictly commercial (cotton, tobacco, and so forth), and number of cashew trees (in logarithmic form) have the expected positive coefficients, but none are statistically significant at the 10 percent level. Similarly, the coefficients for cultivation of horticultural crops and security of land tenure are statistically insignificant.

The variable for citrus and coconut trees has a statistically significant coefficient only in the southern region, where it is probably capturing the importance of oranges, tangerines, and coconuts in Inhambane Province. The coefficients for "other fruit and nut trees" are also positive and significant in the central and southern regions.

The livestock ownership variables are mostly significant, especially in the central and southern regions. The coefficient for large livestock (cattle, goats, sheep) is significant at the 10 percent level in the central region and at the 1 percent level in the south. Livestock herding is less common in the north, where tsetse fly infestation is a problem. The number of fowl owned is significant in all three regions. It is worth noting that this variable is likely to be endogenous, and the causality may run both ways: livestock ownership may increase a household's income and consumption through the sale or consumption of animals and animal products, but better-off households may also purchase livestock as a form of investment.

Infrastructure and Other Community Characteristics

The estimated coefficients for the two infrastructure index variables constructed from

[48]The IAF survey protocol treated unpaid workers differently, depending upon the type of work they did. If the work was in agriculture, they were considered to be employed in the agricultural sector. However, if they reported doing housework (including fetching water or wood, food preparation, and so forth) for their own family, they were not considered as part of the labor force, and not employed in any sector.

the community-level data (one for general economic infrastructure and the other for health services) both have the expected positive signs, but neither is statistically significant. When the economic infrastructure variable is interacted with adult female literacy, the coefficient is positive and significant, suggesting that at least some basic educational background is necessary to realize the benefits of improved economic infrastructure. The other community-level variable, a dummy variable indicating whether malaria was cited as the most important health problem in the community, has an estimated coefficient not significantly different from zero.

Urban Determinants of Consumption and Poverty

Table 7.2 presents the results from the estimation of the urban model of the determinants of real consumption per capita, allowing coefficients to vary between large cities (Maputo, Matola, Beira, and Nampula) and small urban areas. The fit of the model is good, with an adjusted R^2 of 0.491. Results for specific coefficients are discussed below.

Demographic Characteristics

As in the rural model, all of the coefficients on the variables for household size and age composition are large, negative, and statistically significant; the quadratic term for household size is positive and significant. Once again we see the counterintuitive result that the coefficients for adults are more negative than the coefficients for those under the age of 18. As in the rural case, when the model is respecified to allow for economies of household size, the coefficients for age and sex composition of the household remain negative but are slightly smaller when $\theta = 0.8$ and much smaller when $\theta = 0.4$. Also, in the urban model that allows for economies of household size, most of the parameters are unchanged from the model specified in per capita terms, with the exception of the age of the household head and the quadratic term for household size, as was true in the rural reestimation.

In large cities, households with older heads tend to be slightly less poor, with consumption per capita increasing 0.4 percent for each additional year of age; in small urban areas there is no significant relationship between the age of the household head and per capita consumption. In all urban areas, female-headed households are significantly poorer than male-headed households. Other things being equal, the consumption per capita of an urban male-headed household is 17 to 20 percent higher than that of its female-headed counterpart. For urban areas, this result may be seen as reinforcing the results seen in the unconditional poverty profile (in Chapter 2 of MPF/UEM/IFPRI 1998), which showed in a bivariate analysis that in urban areas, female-headed households are more likely to be poor than male-headed households.

The variables for number of persons with disabilities and number of war migrants in the family do not appear to be significant determinants of per capita consumption. The variable for the number of women who had their first child before the age of 16 is significant (at the 10 percent level) and negative only in large cities.

Education

While all estimated coefficients for the education variables have the expected positive signs, they are not always significant. For example, adult male literacy is not a significant explanatory variable in large or small urban areas, nor is female literacy significant in small urban areas. The coefficient for adult female literacy in big cities is extremely large, suggesting an increase in per capita consumption of 25 percent associated with having an additional literate woman in the household.[49]

The adult female primary education coefficients are positive and significant in both large and small urban areas. The corresponding variable for males is positive, but insignificant, for both classifications of urban areas. In each setting the adult female primary education coefficient is larger than the coefficient for males. As in the case of the rural model, the variable for the maximum educational level of anyone in the household is large and significant in both types of urban areas, and it is especially large in the big cities. Also, as in the case of the rural model, the lack of significance of some of the education variables is partly because of their effect being picked up by the significant effect of the maximum education variable.

Employment and Income Sources

In urban areas, the coefficients for employment in the agricultural, industrial, or construction sectors are statistically insignificant, which is a surprising result. On the other hand, employment in the services sector ("other") is significant, positive, and reasonably large in both large and small urban areas. Diversification of income sources does not add any independent explanatory power to the model, with estimated coefficients that are essentially zero.

Agriculture and Livestock

Among the agriculture and livestock variables, area cultivated (in square root transformation) is not a significant determinant of per capita consumption in either large cities or in small urban areas. The use of agricultural equipment or irrigation has the expected positive sign and a relatively large coefficient, and it is significant at the 10 percent level. The land tenure variables did not work as expected: the coefficient is insignificant in the large cities model and has a perverse (and significant) negative sign in small urban areas.

Because of the relative scarcity of tree crops in urban areas, we used a more aggregated variable for tree crops in the urban model. The log of the total number of fruit and nut trees is negative but insignificant in large cities, and positive and significant in small urban areas. Both livestock variables are positive and significant in both types of urban areas. Interestingly, the variable for total tropical livestock unit (TLU) is especially large in big cities, where an additional TLU is associated with 17 percent higher per capita consumption levels. The effect is much smaller in small urban areas. The number of poultry owned is significant at the 10 percent level in large cities and the 1 percent level in small urban areas.

[49]Note that, because the model also controls for household size, the variable really measures the effect on per capita consumption of an adult literate female in the household relative to that same adult female being illiterate.

CHAPTER 8

Poverty Reduction Simulations

Methodology

Having estimated the consumption models, we now move to the task of simulating poverty reduction interventions and estimating the associated change in poverty levels. We illustrate the key steps of the procedure for the headcount index here; the formulae for simulating other poverty measures are given in Appendix 2.

Using the estimated parameters ($\hat{\beta}$) of the preferred model, we first generate predictions of consumption per capita ($\hat{c}_j$) for every household j as

$$\hat{c}_j = e^{(\hat{\beta}' x_j + \hat{\sigma}^2 / 2)} \tag{7}$$

The term $\hat{\sigma}^2 / 2$, where $\hat{\sigma}$ is the estimated standard error of the regression, is required because of the lognormal transformation of the dependent variable (Greene 1997). Corresponding to every predicted consumption level, there is a probability of the household being poor (P_{0j}), which is given by

$$\hat{P}_{0j} = prob(\ln \hat{c}_j < \ln z) = prob(\eta_j < \ln z - \hat{\beta}' x_j) = \Phi[(\ln z - \hat{\beta}' x_j) / \hat{\sigma}], \tag{8}$$

where Φ is the standard normal distribution function, σ is the standard error of the regression, and the circumflex (^) indicates estimated values.

Based on predicted consumption, one could, of course, construct a binary variable to classify a household as poor or nonpoor. But predicted consumption is only a point estimate, which comes with its own prediction or forecast error. Thus, for example, even if predicted consumption were above the poverty line for a given household, there is a nonzero probability that the true value of that household's predicted consumption is below the poverty line. It is therefore appropriate to treat predicted consumption as a stochastic variable, and hence, we go on to compute the probability of being poor associated with any given level of predicted consumption.

Finally, a weighted average of the household probabilities of being poor gives the predicted national headcount index, with the weight for each household being the product of the survey sample weight and the number of members in the household. Predicted measures of the depth and severity of poverty can be derived similarly (see Appendix 2).

The poverty simulations we consider below are based on the parameter estimates of the preferred models. The usual caveat applies to the results of this simulation analysis. The simulations assume that the considered changes in the determinant variables do not affect the model parameters or other exogenous variables. While this is a plausible assumption for incremental changes, it warrants a more cautious interpretation for simulations that involve large policy changes.

Simulations

We now consider a set of policy simulations. The purpose of these simulations is twofold. The first is to illustrate the impact that changes in the levels of the determinants of poverty have on poverty levels. Where explanatory variables are intrinsically related to one another, it is sometimes difficult to trace the relationship between a determinant and the outcome variable by examination of the regression coefficients alone. For example, for households that do not have an adult who has completed primary school (the majority of households in the IAF sample), increasing the number of adult females with EP2 will also increase the maximum educational level attained by any adult in the household; these are two separate variables in the determinants models, and the effect on consumption per capita in these households will be the sum of the two effects. There might be implications for the number of literate persons in the household, too.[50] In the same manner, direct interpretation of the regression coefficients is complicated by the presence of interacted variables.

The second purpose of the simulations is to demonstrate, in a relatively nontechnical fashion, the effects that various policies can have on consumption and poverty. For this reason, we focus on altering variables that are amenable to change, to at least some degree, through public policy.

Before running the simulations, it is necessary to establish a reference point, or base simulation. This is because the empirical models of the determinants of poverty are not perfect predictors of consumption per capita, or poverty; as such, it would be incorrect to compare simulated mean consumption and poverty levels with the actual levels (reported in Chapter 5). Instead, the correct reference points are the means of predicted per capita consumption values ($\hat{c}_j$) and predicted poverty levels ($\hat{P}_{\alpha j}$) obtained from the regressions using the original values for x_j, as per equations (7) and (8), respectively. Table 8.1 compares the actual mean consumption and poverty levels with the results of the base simulations. From the

Table 8.1 Comparison of actual measures of well-being with the base simulation

	Rural		Urban	
Welfare measure	Actual	Base simulation	Actual	Base simulation
Mean daily consumption per capita[a]	4,933.95	4,996.78	6,663.62	6,658.10
Poverty headcount	0.712	0.679	0.620	0.581
Poverty gap	0.299	0.295	0.267	0.263
Squared poverty gap	0.159	0.163	0.146	0.151

[a]Expressed in meticais at temporally and spatially adjusted 1996–97 prices.

[50]One could avoid these complications by assuming that a change in a given variable does not lead to changes in other variables. In the example used here, one could assume that there is already someone in the household with primary education, and that there is someone who is literate and would go on to complete primary education. However, these assumptions often diverge a great deal from reality, and the simulations provide a simple way to avoid making unnecessary, and unrealistic, simplifying assumptions.

table, we see that the predicted mean consumption and poverty measures are close to the actual values calculated from the IAF data, although the headcount index is somewhat lower in the base simulations.

The simulation results are presented in Tables 8.2 through 8.9, with results grouped by the sector of the intervention. These tables show results for the rural, urban, and national populations, showing the change in mean real consumption per capita resulting from the simulated change in the independent variables, and the changes in the three poverty measures corresponding to that change in consumption. The poverty measures capture the distributional effects of the change in consumption from the simulation. For each set of interventions, separate tables show the impact on the total population and on the subset of the population that is directly affected by the intervention.

One result that is common to almost all of the simulations is that the percentage change in the poverty indexes is greater for higher orders of P_α. That is, the percentage reduction in the poverty gap is generally larger than the reduction in the headcount index, and the reduction in the squared poverty gap is generally larger than the reduction in the poverty gap. This is, at least in part, because although many of these simulations raise the consumption levels of the poor, they do not always move the poor from below the poverty line to above the poverty line. This, in turn, may be because the increase in consumption is small, or because the households in question are far below the poverty to begin with, or both. Nevertheless, improving the well-being of those remaining below the poverty line is still an important consideration, especially in a country such as Mozambique, where two-thirds of the population is below the poverty line.

When examining the simulation results, it is useful to bear in mind that magnitude of change in mean consumption and poverty in each of the simulations is attributable to three factors: the quantitative relationship between the determinant of poverty and per capita consumption (that is, the sign and magnitude of the regression coefficients), the size of the considered change in the determinant of poverty (that is, the magnitude of the simulated change in the X_j variables), and the proportion of the population affected by the simulation. Moreover, as the approach used here is primarily partial equilibrium in nature, general equilibrium effects are taken into account only to the limited extent that a reduced form approach captures such effects. Relative to a structural general equilibrium model, the results presented here could overstate or understate the impact of the interventions on poverty reduction.

Education

In simulations 1–5, we present the effects of increased educational levels on per capita consumption and poverty (Tables 8.2 and 8.3). Simulations 1 and 2 focus on basic literacy, whereas simulations 3 to 5 explore the effects of increased rates of primary school completion (EP2). For simulation 1, we increased, by one, the number of adult males in the household who could read and write; this change only applies to households where there is at least one adult male who cannot read and write. Eighteen percent of the urban population lives in such households, compared with 46 percent of the rural population (Table 8.3). Based on the IAF data, this simulation would have the effect of increasing the urban adult male literacy rate from 83 to 99 percent, while in rural areas the adult male literacy rate would almost double, from 50 percent to 95 percent. For the entire population, mean consumption per capita increases by 4 percent in rural areas and 1 percent in urban areas (Table 8.2). The increase in consumption per capita is distributed such that it reduces the poverty headcount by 3 percent in rural areas and 1 percent in urban areas. The percentage changes in the average poverty gap (P_1) and squared poverty gap (P_2) are greater than the changes in the headcount.

Table 8.2 Education simulation results: Total changes in consumption and poverty levels

Simulation number	Description	Percent change in mean consumption per capita			Percent change in poverty headcount (P_0)			Percent change in poverty gap (P_1)			Percent change in squared poverty gap (P_2)		
		Rural	Urban	National	Rural	Urban	National	Rural	Urban	National	Rural	Urban	National
1	Increase by 1 the number of literate adult males in the household	4.3	0.9	3.4	–3.3	–0.9	–2.8	–5.6	–1.7	–4.9	–7.2	–2.4	–6.3
2	Increase by 1 the number of literate adult females in the household	8.1	9.9	8.5	–6.4	–10.1	–7.1	–10.9	–17.4	–12.1	–13.9	–22.3	–15.5
3	Increase by 1 the number of adult males in the household with EP2, if there are any adult males with less than EP2.[a]	15.3	14.6	15.2	–11.7	–13.5	–12.0	–18.4	–20.8	–18.9	–22.7	–25.5	–23.2
4	Increase by 1 the number of adult females in the household with EP2, if there are any adult females with less than EP2.[a]	26.8	29.9	27.6	–20.5	–26.8	–21.6	–30.8	–38.8	–32.3	–37.0	–46.0	–38.8
5	At least one adult in the household has EP2 level of education.[a]	22.7	20.3	22.1	–17.1	–19.0	–17.4	–26.0	–29.0	–26.5	–31.4	–35.3	–32.2

Note: For purposes of calculating the national impact, nonapplicable simulations are treated as having zero impact on consumption and poverty in urban areas.
[a]EP2 indicates a full primary education (seven years).

Table 8.3 Education simulation results (affected subpopulation only)

Simulation	Percent of population affected			Percent change in mean consumption per capita			Percent change in poverty headcount (P_0)			Percent change in poverty gap (P_1)			Percent change in squared poverty gap (P_2)		
number	Rural	Urban	National	Rural	Urban	National	Rural	Urban	National	Rural	Urban	National	Rural	Urban	National
1	46.4	18.3	40.7	9.9	7.1	9.4	–6.7	–3.9	–6.1	–10.9	–6.8	–10.1	–13.6	–8.7	–12.6
2	86.7	50.0	79.2	9.8	28.2	13.5	–7.2	–16.2	–9.0	–12.0	–25.6	–14.7	–15.1	–31.2	–18.4
3	87.2	71.9	84.1	18.1	22.8	19.0	–13.1	–17.5	–14.0	–20.5	–26.5	–21.7	–25.1	–32.1	–26.5
4	97.2	88.2	95.3	28.3	37.8	30.2	–20.7	–28.6	–22.3	–31.1	–40.9	–33.1	–37.4	–48.1	–39.6
5	92.6	56.3	85.2	25.0	47.6	29.6	–18.2	–28.3	–20.3	–27.4	–40.6	–30.1	–33.0	–47.7	–36.0

For instance, the rural poverty gap and squared poverty gap indexes decline by 6 and 7 percent, respectively.

In Table 8.3, we see that among the households affected by this simulation, the corresponding changes for the simulation are larger, as must be the case. Among affected households, rural mean consumption increases by 10 percent and urban by 7 percent, while the rural and urban headcount indexes decline by 7 and 4 percent, respectively.

Simulation 2 is the corresponding simulation for adult females. Because there are greater numbers of households with adult females who are not literate, this simulation affects a much larger population than does the simulation for male literacy: an estimated 87 percent of the rural population and 50 percent of the urban population live in households where there is at least one adult female who cannot read and write (Table 8.3). Simulation 2 would increase the female literacy rate from its present levels of 15 percent in rural areas and 57 percent in urban areas, to 86 and 95 percent, respectively. This large change, combined with regression coefficients that are typically higher for female literacy than male literacy (see Tables 7.1 and 7.2), leads to a much greater impact on consumption and poverty than occurs in simulation 1, especially in urban areas. As shown in Table 8.2, mean per capita consumption increases by 8 percent in rural areas and 10 percent in urban areas, while the poverty headcounts in the two zones decline by 6 and 10 percent, respectively, with even greater percentage reductions in the higher-order poverty indexes. Note that the percentage reduction in poverty is greater in urban areas, despite the fact that the simulation affects a smaller proportion of the urban population than it does the rural population.

Simulations 3 and 4 are similar to simulations 1 and 2, except that they model the effects of increasing educational attainment of adult males and females at a higher, and necessarily formal, level: completion of primary school (seven years of schooling). As seen in Table 8.3, these simulations affect the large majority of the population, meaning that a high proportion of the population lives in households where there is at least one adult male (simulation 3) or adult female (simulation 4) who has not completed primary school. Note that the changes implied by simulations 3 and 4 are enormous. According to the IAF data, only 4 percent of rural adult males and 20 percent of urban adult males have completed full primary education. Under simulation 3 those rates would change to 86 and 81 percent, respectively. The changes implied by simulation 4 are even more dramatic, with the percentage of adult women who have completed primary school increasing from 1 percent to 80 percent in rural areas and from 11 to 80 percent in urban areas. Because the change is so large, these results should be treated with extra caution.

As one would expect, primary schooling has a larger impact on per capita consumption than literacy alone does.[51] For simulation 3, which changes the educational level of one adult male from below full primary to complete primary schooling, the effects are roughly equal in rural and urban areas, with increases in mean consumption per capita of about 15 percent.

[51]Note that for the simulations, in households where there was a person of the appropriate sex who was literate but had not completed primary school, we simply increased the value of the primary school completion variable and, if necessary, the value of the variable for the maximum level of education in the family. However, if none of those who had not completed primary school were literate, we also increased the literacy variable by one, as one cannot be illiterate and complete primary school successfully. Thus, the effect of primary school completion on per capita consumption is often the sum of several regression coefficients, rather than the coefficient for primary school completion alone.

Overall, there is a reduction in the poverty headcount of 12 percent, and in the poverty gap and squared poverty gap of about 19 and 23 percent, respectively (Table 8.2).

As with literacy, the effects of increased female primary school completion (simulation 4) are greater than those for males, because a (marginally) greater proportion of the population is affected, and more important, because the estimated return to female primary education is higher than that for male primary education (see the estimated regression coefficients in Tables 7.1 and 7.2). Overall, the impact of simulation 4 is almost twice as large as simulation 3 for all measures shown in Table 8.2.

Simulation 5 uses a different approach to simulating the effects of a change in educational levels on consumption and poverty. In this case, we simulate the effect of guaranteeing that at least one adult in the household, male or female, completes primary school. According to the IAF data, in 1996–97, 38 percent of urban households and only 6 percent of rural households had a member who had completed a full primary education. As might be expected, the effect of this simulation on poverty and consumption falls somewhere between those for simulations 3 and 4. In percentage terms, the poverty-reducing effects of such a policy are approximately equal in rural and urban areas (Table 8.2).

Agriculture

We examine the agricultural determinants of poverty by altering several different variables representing different approaches to agriculture-based policies to reduce poverty. These include expanding the area cultivated per household, increasing the use of productivity-enhancing agricultural inputs, increasing the productivity (or number) of fruit and nut trees, increasing the production of crops that are exclusively commercial (for example, cotton or tea), increasing the livestock holdings of households that own livestock, and promoting wider ownership of livestock across households. The agriculture simulations for the entire population are shown in Table 8.4, with results for the affected population appearing in Table 8.5.

Simulation 6 estimates the effect of increasing, by 0.5 hectares, the cropping area operated by those households who already have at least some agricultural land.[52] As may be seen in Table 8.5, this change would affect one-half of the urban population and nearly all of the rural population. Even though the proportion of the population affected is extremely large, the impact on consumption and poverty is small, with Table 8.4 showing less than a 1 percent increase in mean consumption per capita, a less than 1 percent reduction in the poverty headcount, and similarly meager reductions in the other poverty measures. As an addition of 0.5 hectare of land per household is not a small change—recall that the average land size reported by landholders is 2.4 hectares—then clearly the limited magnitude of the change can be attributed to the small coefficient on the land variable, which was noted earlier in the discussion of the regression results.

Simulation 7 takes a more targeted approach to increasing area cultivated. The increase in total land cultivated is approximately the same as in simulation 6, but in this case it is an increase of 1 hectare per household, targeted to those households

[52]Unlike many countries in Sub-Saharan Africa, in many (but certainly not all) parts of Mozambique there is unused arable land. In these areas it is not so much the land constraint that is binding for farmers, but rather the labor constraint, with the area cultivated limited by the amount of labor and labor-saving technology available to clear and work additional land. It is estimated that the magnitude of the additional cultivation implied by these simulations, while large, can be met from land that is not presently farmed.

Table 8.4 Agriculture simulation results: Total changes in consumption and poverty levels

Simulation number	Description	Percent change in mean consumption per capita			Percent change in poverty headcount (P_0)			Percent change in poverty gap (P_1)			Percent change in squared poverty gap (P_2)		
		Rural	Urban	National	Rural	Urban	National	Rural	Urban	National	Rural	Urban	National
6	Increase agricultural holdings by 0.5 hectares among households who presently have any agricultural land	0.5	0.3	0.4	−0.4	−0.3	−0.4	−0.6	−0.4	−0.6	−0.8	−0.5	−0.7
7	Increase agricultural holdings by 1 hectare among households who presently have agricultural land of 2 hectares or less	0.4	0.3	0.4	−0.3	−0.3	−0.3	−0.5	−0.4	−0.5	−0.6	−0.5	−0.6
8	Households with 1 hectare or less adopt irrigation and agricultural inputs	1.8	2.3	1.9	−1.4	−2.2	−1.5	−2.0	−3.6	−2.3	−2.4	−4.6	−2.8
9	Households with land up to 2 hectares adopt irrigation and agricultural inputs	3.7	3.3	3.6	−2.9	−3.2	−2.9	−4.3	−5.4	−4.5	−5.2	−6.8	−5.5
10	Households with any land adopt irrigation and agricultural inputs	5.2	4.1	4.9	−4.1	−3.9	−4.0	−6.6	−6.5	−6.6	−8.3	−8.2	−8.3
11	Increase number of cashew trees by 20 percent	0.0	n.a.	0.0	0.0	n.a.	0.0	0.0	n.a.	0.0	0.0	n.a.	0.0
12	Increase the number of farmers growing cashew in main cashew growing areas	0.8	n.a.	0.6	−0.6	n.a.	−0.5	−1.0	n.a.	−0.8	−1.1	n.a.	−0.9
13	Increase citrus production by 20 percent	0.1	n.a.	0.1	−0.1	n.a.	0.0	−0.1	n.a.	−0.1	−0.1	n.a.	−0.1
14	Households currently producing basic food crops or horticultural crops start producing commercial crops	3.1	n.a.	2.3	−2.4	n.a.	−2.0	−4.0	n.a.	−3.3	−5.0	n.a.	−4.1
15	Increase number of poultry by 50 percent (among those having poultry)	1.4	0.7	1.2	−0.9	−0.4	−0.9	−1.6	−0.6	−1.4	−2.0	−0.6	−1.7
16	Increase number of tropical livestock units (TLU) by 50 percent	0.5	0.5	0.5	−0.2	−0.3	−0.2	−0.4	−0.4	−0.4	−0.4	−0.5	−0.4
17	Give median poultry to those without	1.0	1.4	1.1	−0.8	−1.3	−0.9	−1.3	−2.0	−1.4	−1.7	−2.4	−1.8
18	Give median TLU to those without	0.7	n.a.	0.5	−0.6	n.a.	−0.4	−0.9	n.a.	−0.7	−1.1	n.a.	−0.9

Notes: n.a. indicates that the simulation does not apply to urban areas. For purposes of calculating the national impact, nonapplicable simulations are treated as having zero impact on consumption and poverty in urban areas.

Table 8.5 Agriculture simulation results (affected subpopulation only)

Simulation	Percent of population affected			Percent change in mean consumption per capita			Percent change in poverty headcount (P_0)			Percent change in poverty gap (P_1)			Percent change in squared poverty gap (P_2)		
number	Rural	Urban	National	Rural	Urban	National	Rural	Urban	National	Rural	Urban	National	Rural	Urban	National
6	95.4	52.1	86.6	0.5	0.6	0.5	–0.4	–0.4	–0.4	–0.6	–0.6	–0.6	–0.8	–0.7	–0.8
7	61.2	40.0	56.9	0.7	0.9	0.7	–0.6	–0.6	–0.6	–0.9	–0.9	–0.9	–1.0	–1.1	–1.1
8	28.5	24.0	27.6	5.9	12.0	7.1	–5.3	–7.9	–5.8	–8.0	–12.5	–8.9	–9.7	–15.4	–10.8
9	59.4	35.3	54.5	5.9	12.0	7.1	–5.0	–7.7	–5.5	–7.8	–12.1	–8.7	–9.6	–14.9	–10.7
10	89.3	43.2	80.0	5.9	12.0	7.1	–4.5	–7.7	–5.2	–7.3	–12.1	–8.3	–9.0	–14.9	–10.2
11	23.6	n.a.	18.8	0.1	n.a.	0.1	–0.1	n.a.	–0.1	–0.2	n.a.	–0.1	–0.2	n.a.	–0.2
12	18.4	n.a.	14.7	3.8	n.a.	3.1	–3.3	n.a.	–2.6	–5.4	n.a.	–4.3	–6.7	n.a.	–5.3
13	22.5	n.a.	17.9	0.3	n.a.	0.2	–0.3	n.a.	–0.2	–0.5	n.a.	–0.4	–0.7	n.a.	–0.5
14	90.5	n.a.	72.1	3.5	n.a.	2.8	–2.6	n.a.	–2.1	–4.4	n.a.	–3.5	–5.5	n.a.	–4.4
15	56.4	19.5	48.9	2.5	3.3	2.6	–1.7	–2.3	–1.8	–2.8	–3.0	–2.8	–3.5	–3.3	–3.5
16	25.8	7.0	22.0	1.4	7.4	2.7	–0.8	–4.0	–1.5	–1.3	–5.8	–2.2	–1.6	–7.1	–2.7
17	43.6	80.5	51.1	2.3	1.8	2.2	–1.8	–1.6	–1.8	–3.0	–2.4	–2.9	–3.8	–3.0	–3.7
18	79.5	n.a.	63.3	0.9	n.a.	0.7	–0.7	n.a.	–0.6	–1.1	n.a.	–0.9	–1.4	n.a.	–1.1

Note: n.a. indicates that the simulation does not apply to urban areas. For purposes of calculating the national impact, nonapplicable simulations are treated as having zero impact on consumption and poverty in urban areas.

who presently have 2 hectares or less. Even though this simulation affects fewer households, the results are essentially the same as those for simulation 7 (Table 8.4).

Simulations 8–10 examine the effects of increasing the use of one or more productivity-enhancing agricultural inputs, including fertilizers, pesticides, heavy equipment, and irrigation. The three simulations consider the same change in the independent variable: the dummy variable for use of modern agricultural inputs is changed from zero to one, limited to those who were cultivating at least some land at the time of the survey. The difference is in the group selected for the change. In simulation 8, the change is limited to those households that have some land but no more than 1 hectare; this simulation applies to 29 percent of the rural population and 24 percent of the urban population (Table 8.5). In simulation 9, the upper limit on landholding size is relaxed to include all households with no more than 2 hectares; this simulation affects 59 percent of the rural population and 35 percent of the urban population. Finally, simulation 10 includes all households cultivating some land at the time of the survey—89 percent of the rural sample and 43 percent of the urban sample.

As shown in Table 8.5, in each of the simulations 8–10, the mean per capita consumption of the affected population increases by 6 percent in rural areas and 12 percent in urban areas, which is considerably higher than the results for the land expansion simulations (simulations 6 and 7). This suggests that productivity-enhancing inputs are likely to have a larger impact on consumption and poverty than land expansion will. However, in Table 8.4, even in the most ambitious case (simulation 10), in which all farming households adopt at least some modern agricultural technology, the gains in consumption per capita are modest, at about 5 percent, and reductions in the poverty headcount are similarly modest at 4 percent.

Simulations 11 and 12 explore the effects of expanded production of cashew nuts, formerly a major export earner for Mozambique, and a subject of considerable policy interest in recent years as the country tries to revive the industry. One area of focus has been to increase the productivity of existing cashew trees by rehabilitating the existing stock of trees, which is the primary avenue for increasing cashew nut production in the short term (World Bank and Ministry of Agriculture and Fisheries 1998; Mole 2000). Another approach is to increase the number of trees that each cashew producer has in production, although that approach is inherently medium to long term, as cashew trees do not start producing nuts in any significant quantity until five to six years after planting. Simulation 11 captures either of these approaches to expanding cashew production by simulating a 20 percent increase in cashew production among existing cashew producers: the simulation is general enough that it could be interpreted as increased production of existing trees or the planting of new trees by current cashew growers. The simulation is limited to rural areas because urban cashew production is negligible. In Table 8.4 we see that there is almost no impact on mean consumption levels or on poverty. In part, this is because of the relatively small population affected by the simulation; that is, the small proportion of the population living in households that currently grow cashews (Table 8.5). It is also because the estimated coefficients in the relationship between the number of cashew trees and per capita consumption are small; the impact is almost zero even among those affected by the simulation.

A different approach to expanding cashew production, currently being promoted, is to encourage households to begin producing cashews, which is modeled in Simulation 12. We selected a random sample of 50 percent of households in the main cashew-producing provinces (Nampula, Zambézia, Gaza, and Inhambane) that were not growing cashews at the time of the survey, and "gave" each household 46 cashew trees—twice the median number of cashew trees calculated from the sample of cashew producers in those provinces. The large number of trees and high proportion of new growers were chosen because earlier simulations (not presented here but available from the authors upon request) with more conservative growth in new cashew producers had a small impact. Even this large increase had a small impact on affected households (Table 8.5) and a much smaller impact on mean consumption and poverty at the national level (Table 8.4).[53]

Simulation 13 examines the potential poverty-reducing impact of expanded production of citrus fruit or coconut; coconut was included because it is economically important for both income and home consumption in the coastal zones of Zambézia and Inhambane provinces. As with the first cashew simulation (simulation 11), we model a 20 percent increase in citrus and coconut production and also limit the simulation to rural areas. Here, too, the impact on consumption and poverty is negligible, for those affected by the simulation as well as the country at large (Tables 8.4 and 8.5).

Simulation 14 examines crop selection, modeling the effects on households who are currently producing any type of crop and adopting crops that may be considered strictly commercial, as defined in Chapter 6.[54] Note that the simulation specifies adoption of commercial crops in addition to the crops the household was already producing. Most (although not all) of these crops are not suitable for production in urban environments, so the simulation is limited to rural areas, where it affects 91 percent of the population (that is, 9 percent of the rural population was in households that were already growing one or more of these crops). In this simulation, mean consumption increases by 3 percent and the poverty headcount in rural areas declines by 2 percent. Reductions in the other poverty measures are greater, with the poverty gap declining by 4 percent and the squared poverty gap dropping by 5 percent.

The final agriculture simulation looks at the relationship between poverty and livestock ownership. Here the relationship shown in the simulations needs to be treated with extra caution, because while livestock can be used as an asset that can generate returns and raise incomes, they are also a reflection of past income gains. In simulations 15 and 16, we simulate increases in livestock ownership among the subset of households that already own livestock. Specifically, we increase the number of poultry owned by 50 percent (simulation 15) and the number of TLU (which cover cattle, sheep, goats, and pigs) by 50 percent (simulation 16). In Table 8.4, we see that the total impact on consumption and poverty is small in both urban and rural areas, with mean consumption per capita increasing by only 1 percent for the poultry simulation, and less than 1 percent for

[53]In the IAF data, there are 2,629 rural households in those four provinces, of which 1,006 had cashew trees at the time of the survey, with a median number of 23 trees per cashew-producing household. There were 1,623 households without cashew trees, from which 812 households were randomly selected. As the simulation results depend in part upon which 812 households are randomly selected (for example, because the estimated parameters vary by region, and the regional composition of the new growers in the simulation can change with each random draw), we repeated the simulation several times and compared results. None of those exercises showed a large impact on consumption or poverty.

[54]It is possible that some output from some of these crops might be consumed at home, but the processing requirements indicate that such use would most likely be minor. It is also recognized that some of the most important "commercial" crops in Mozambique are basic food crops such as maize. These crops are deliberately excluded from the simulation because of the difficulty in analyzing the dual roles of these crops using the IAF data.

larger livestock. Poverty reductions are correspondingly small for all three poverty measures (Table 8.4). Part of the reason for the small impact is that simulation 15 only affects about one-half of the population (56 percent in rural areas and 20 percent in urban areas). The target population is even smaller for simulation 16, which only reaches 26 percent of the rural population and 7 percent of the urban population (Table 8.5).

Simulations 17 and 18 target those households that do not own poultry or other livestock, examining the potential impact on poverty of increasing the number of households that own livestock. In simulation 17, households that do not own poultry are "given" the median number of poultry in their region; simulation 18 models the analogous expansion of ownership of larger animals. The impact of both simulations is small. As seen in Table 8.4, the impact of wider poultry ownership is approximately the same as the earlier poultry simulation, with consumption increases and poverty index decreases on the order of only 1–2 percent. For the larger livestock (simulation 18), the impact is surprisingly small, given that it affects the 80 percent of the rural population that does not own any cattle, sheep, goats, or pigs (Table 8.5).[55]

Demographic Change

In the poverty profile in MPF/UEM/ IFPRI (1998, Chapter 2) and in the discussion of the results of the regression models in Chapter 7, a negative relationship between household size and consumption per capita was noted. For public policy, household size is most germane in the context of fertility, and Mozambique's National Population Policy (Mozambique, Council of Ministers 1999). In the next set of simulations, we examine the effects of increasing the household size by one member, with that member being a child under the age of 10 (simulation 19), or a working-age male (simulation 20), or a working-age female (simulation 21). As the determinants model also includes information about the educational level and sector of employment of adult household members, in simulations 20 and 21 we assume that the additional household member would have educational characteristics matching those of adults of that sex already in the household and employment characteristics of all adults in the household (as the employment variables in the model are not disaggregated by sex). For example, if a household has one adult female, who has a primary school education, and all adults are employed in the agricultural sector, in simulation 21 it is assumed that the additional adult female also has a primary education and is employed in the agricultural sector. If there is more than one adult female in the household, the additional adult female is assigned the average educational characteristics of all the adult females in the household. By design, these three simulations affect all households in the sample; therefore, there is no need to present results separately for the affected subpopulation, and all results for these simulations appear in Table 8.6.

In Table 8.6, we see that for the most part, increasing household size has a negative impact on consumption per capita and leads to increased poverty. This is especially true in the case of additional children, which is consistent with Eastwood and Lipton's (1999) cross-country study that found higher fertility rates associated with higher poverty rates. In simulations 19–21, the age or sex of the additional person changes only the magnitude of the impact and not the direction. The negative impact of an additional child is similar in rural and urban areas, with mean consumption per capita declining by about 15 percent and the

[55]Simulation 18 is not run for urban households, as a sizable expansion of large livestock herding is clearly not feasible in urban areas.

poverty headcount increasing by approximately 12 percent in both areas. An additional adult female has a smaller negative impact than an additional child, reducing mean consumption per capita by 10 percent and increasing the poverty headcount by 9 percent in rural areas; in urban areas, the corresponding numbers are a 9 percent drop in mean consumption per capita and an 8 percent increase in the poverty headcount. The negative impact of an additional adult male is slightly smaller than that of an additional adult female (Table 8.6).

In view of this critical dependence of the relationship between poverty and household size on the assumption about economies of size, simulations similar to simulations 19–21 are run that incorporate the notion of economies of household size. In practice, the model is reestimated, changing the dependent variable from consumption per capita (which assumes zero economies of household size) to consumption per "equivalent adult" (Lanjouw and Ravallion 1995), using the elasticity of household size at which household size is more or less orthogonal to poverty ($\theta = 0.4$),[56] and an elasticity that is plausible for a country such as Mozambique ($\theta = 0.8$).

When the effects of household size on poverty are purged (simulations 19a–21a) in Table 8.7, the results are more consistent with intuition than the results in simulations 19–21 in Table 8.6. In simulations 19–21, an additional household member reduces consumption per capita and increases poverty in almost all cases, even if the additional person is of working age (and thus, the addition of the member reduces the dependency ratio). When the relationship between poverty and household size is eliminated (by setting θ to 0.4), the impact on well-being of an additional household member is still negative if the additional member is a child (that is, the dependency ratio is increased) as in simulation 19a. However, when the additional member is an adult male (simulation 20a), there is a small increase in consumption per equivalent adult and virtually no change in rural poverty (but a slight increase in urban poverty). When the additional member is an adult female (simulation 21a), mean consumption per equivalent adult increases by approximately 5 percent, and rural poverty drops by 3 to 4 percent, depending upon the index used. Both simulations 20a and 21a show increases in urban poverty, according to the P_1 and P_2 measures, despite the increases in mean consumption. This can occur if the urban gains go mostly to those at or above the poverty line, and those below the poverty line, especially the poorest households, experience reductions in per capita consumption. The reason behind these differential effects in urban areas is not yet clear.

Simulations 19b–21b repeat the analysis with a plausible value for θ, where there are some economies of scale associated with household size, but the economies are small because of the preponderance of privately consumed goods (for example, food) in the consumption bundles of most Mozambicans. As expected, these results reflect an intermediate position between simulations 19–21 and 19a–21a, showing the positive correlation between poverty and household size, even when some account is taken of economies of scale.

Infrastructure Development

Our final simulations explore the potential contributions to poverty reduction of infrastructure development and improved

[56]Note also from previous discussion that economies of household size in Mozambique are unlikely to be as great as that implied by $\theta = 0.4$. However, we use this value because the "true" elasticity of household size is unknown, and because this value eliminates the effect of any relationship between household size and poverty, allowing us to focus on aspects of household composition.

Table 8.6 Demographic change simulation results: Total changes in consumption and poverty levels

Simulation number	Description	Percent change in mean consumption per capita			Percent change in poverty headcount (P_0)			Percent change in poverty gap (P_1)			Percent change in squared poverty gap (P_2)		
		Rural	Urban	National	Rural	Urban	National	Rural	Urban	National	Rural	Urban	National
19	Adding a child	–15.3	–14.6	–15.1	12.5	12.0	12.4	19.1	17.9	18.9	23.0	21.9	22.8
20	Adding a male aged 18–59	–8.3	–8.2	–8.3	7.1	8.0	7.3	9.4	14.8	10.4	10.4	19.8	12.2
21	Adding a female aged 18–59	–10.4	–8.8	–10.0	9.0	8.5	8.9	13.7	16.6	14.2	16.4	22.8	17.6

Table 8.7 Simulated effects of demographic changes, assuming economies of household size

Simulation number	Description	Percent change in mean consumption per capita			Percent change in poverty headcount (P_0)			Percent change in poverty gap (P_1)			Percent change in squared poverty gap (P_2)		
		Rural	Urban	National	Rural	Urban	National	Rural	Urban	National	Rural	Urban	National
	$\theta = 0.4$												
19a	Adding a child	–3.0	–3.9	–3.2	3.2	4.3	3.4	5.4	6.5	5.6	6.8	8.1	7.0
20a	Adding a male aged 18–59	1.1	2.9	1.5	–0.3	0.2	–0.2	0.0	3.4	0.7	0.1	6.1	1.3
21a	Adding a female aged 18–59	5.2	4.3	5.0	–2.9	–0.4	–2.4	–3.6	4.3	–2.0	–4.0	8.4	–1.5
	$\theta = 0.8$												
19b	Adding a child	–11.1	–10.9	–11.0	9.9	9.8	9.9	15.4	14.9	15.3	18.8	18.2	18.7
20b	Adding a male aged 18–59	–7.5	–4.4	–6.9	7.0	5.8	6.8	10.7	11.7	10.9	12.7	16.3	13.4
21b	Adding a female aged 18–59	–5.1	–4.3	–5.0	5.5	5.9	5.6	8.8	13.2	9.7	10.6	19.0	12.3

physical access to health services. We do this using the two infrastructure index variables described in Chapter 6—one for general economic infrastructure and one for health services infrastructure. The simulation is limited to rural areas, as these variables (derived from the rural community questionnaire) were not collected in urban areas. In either of the two simulations, we set a minimum value for the infrastructure index at twice the overall mean value of the index. For the economic infrastructure index, this implies raising the minimum index value to 0.292 and the mean from 0.146 to 0.319. For the health infrastructure index, the minimum value is raised to 0.212, and the mean is raised from 0.106 to 0.270. This implies an ambitious and widespread infrastructure development program, but it will be recalled that these communities were recovering from the protracted war, so they are starting from a low base. These simulations affect approximately 80 percent of the rural population, although to varying degrees, as initial values of the indexes take a range of values from zero to one, inclusive.

Simulation 22 models the increase in the economic infrastructure index, which captures the presence of any of the following in a community: a bank, a market, a paved or improved earthen road, an agricultural extension office, a post office, and a public telephone. In this simulation, mean consumption per capita increases by 3 percent, and poverty declines by 2 to 5 percent, with the largest poverty reductions occurring among the poorest households (Table 8.8). This occurs in part because the increase in the *X* variable is greatest for those villages that currently have the lowest level of services. Improvements in the health services infrastructure (simulation 23) have a much smaller impact on poverty than the economic infrastructure improvements modeled in simulation 22. This is mainly because the relationship between the health services infrastructure and consumption per capita is much weaker (with a regression coefficient of only 0.052). The change for the affected population is shown in Table 8.9.

Sensitivity Analysis

As discussed in Chapter 6 and in this chapter, the analysis presented here—like most such analyses—involves numerous decisions about specific methodological practices. While we believe these decisions are sound, it is nevertheless important to assess how robust the results are to reasonable variations in methodology. In this section we specifically take up two alternatives discussed earlier: using consumption per AEU as a welfare measure instead of consumption per capita, and using poverty lines that are derived using a uniform food bundle throughout the country, rather than region-specific food bundles. We also present results regarding the precision of the simulation estimates, in the form of point estimates and standard errors for mean consumption and the three main poverty indexes , P_0, P_1, and P_2. The standard errors are adjusted for the complex sample design of the survey. Tables 8.10 through 8.15 compare the results for each of the simulations, disaggregated by rural or urban zone of residence. As a convenient shorthand, we refer to the three methods being compared as MB (multiple, region-specific food bundles and consumption per capita)(Tables 8.10–8.11), AEU (multiple, region-specific food bundles and consumption per AEU)(Tables 8.12–8.13), and SB (single, national bundle and consumption per capita)(Tables 8.14–8.15).

It is important to note at the outset that because this analysis varies the dependent variable, the mean value of the dependent variable changes for each method. The clearest case is comparing either of the per capita measures (MB or SB) with AEU: virtually all households have more people than AEUs, so consumption per AEU is higher than consumption per capita. An analogous but subtler difference appears between MB

Table 8.8 Infrastructure simulation results: Total changes in consumption and poverty levels

Simulation number	Description	Percent change in mean consumption per capita			Percent change in poverty headcount (P_0)			Percent change in poverty gap (P_1)			Percent change in squared poverty gap (P_2)		
		Rural	Urban	National	Rural	Urban	National	Rural	Urban	National	Rural	Urban	National
22	Improving economic infrastructure in the community	3.2	n.a.	2.5	−2.5	n.a.	−2.0	−4.0	n.a.	−3.2	−4.9	n.a.	−3.9
23	Improving health facilities in the community	0.8	n.a.	0.7	−0.7	n.a.	−0.5	−1.1	n.a.	−0.9	−1.4	n.a.	−1.1

Note: n.a. indicates that the simulation does not apply to urban areas. For purposes of calculating the national impact, nonapplicable simulations are treated as having zero impact on consumption and poverty in urban areas.

Table 8.9 Infrastructure simulation results (affected subpopulation only)

Simulation number	Percent of population affected			Percent change in mean consumption per capita			Percent change in poverty headcount (P_0)			Percent change in poverty gap (P_1)			Percent change in squared poverty gap (P_2)		
	Rural	Urban	National	Rural	Urban	National	Rural	Urban	National	Rural	Urban	National	Rural	Urban	National
22	79.2	n.a.	63.2	4.0	n.a.	3.2	−3.1	n.a.	−2.5	−5.0	n.a.	−4.0	−6.2	n.a.	−4.9
23	77.8	n.a.	62.0	1.1	n.a.	0.9	−0.9	n.a.	−0.7	−1.4	n.a.	−1.1	−1.8	n.a.	−1.4

Note: n.a. indicates that the simulation does not apply to urban areas. For purposes of calculating the national impact, nonapplicable simulations are treated as having zero impact on consumption and poverty in urban areas.

Table 8.10 Means, standard errors, and percentage change of simulated consumption and poverty indexes: Rural areas using consumption per capita and region-specific food bundles

	Consumption		P_0		P_1		P_2	
Simulation number	Mean (SE)	Percent change	Mean (SE)	Percent change	Mean (SE)	Percent change	Mean (SE)	Percent change
Base	4,997 (125)		0.679 (0.014)		0.295 (0.011)		0.163 (0.008)	
1	5,210 (132)	4.3	0.657 (0.015)	–3.3	0.279 (0.011)	–5.6	0.151 (0.008)	–7.2
2	5,400 (145)	8.1	0.635 (0.016)	–6.4	0.263 (0.011)	–10.9	0.140 (0.008)	–13.9
3	5,764 (223)	15.3	0.600 (0.023)	–11.7	0.241 (0.015)	–18.4	0.126 (0.010)	–22.7
4	6,336 (374)	26.8	0.540 (0.037)	–20.5	0.204 (0.021)	–30.8	0.103 (0.013)	–37.0
5	6,130 (254)	22.7	0.563 (0.025)	–17.1	0.219 (0.015)	–26.0	0.112 (0.010)	–31.4
6	5,022 (126)	0.5	0.677 (0.014)	–0.4	0.294 (0.011)	–0.6	0.162 (0.008)	–0.8
7	5,019 (126)	0.4	0.677 (0.014)	–0.3	0.294 (0.011)	–0.5	0.162 (0.008)	–0.6
8	5,089 (151)	1.8	0.670 (0.016)	–1.4	0.289 (0.012)	–2.0	0.159 (0.009)	–2.4
9	5,179 (196)	3.7	0.660 (0.021)	–2.9	0.283 (0.015)	–4.3	0.154 (0.010)	–5.2
10	5,257 (239)	5.2	0.652 (0.026)	–4.1	0.276 (0.018)	–6.6	0.149 (0.012)	–8.3
11	4,998 (125)	0.0	0.679 (0.014)	0.0	0.295 (0.011)	0.0	0.163 (0.008)	0.0
12	5,036 (124)	0.8	0.675 (0.014)	–0.6	0.293 (0.011)	–1.0	0.161 (0.008)	–1.1
13	5,001 (125)	0.1	0.679 (0.014)	–0.1	0.295 (0.011)	–0.1	0.163 (0.008)	–0.1
14	5,151 (223)	3.1	0.663 (0.024)	–2.4	0.284 (0.018)	–4.0	0.155 (0.013)	–5.0
15	5,066 (129)	1.4	0.673 (0.014)	–0.9	0.291 (0.011)	–1.6	0.160 (0.008)	–2.0
16	5,021 (126)	0.5	0.678 (0.014)	–0.2	0.294 (0.011)	–0.4	0.162 (0.008)	–0.4
17	5,047 (127)	1.0	0.674 (0.014)	–0.8	0.291 (0.011)	–1.3	0.160 (0.008)	–1.7
18	5,032 (128)	0.7	0.675 (0.014)	–0.6	0.293 (0.011)	–0.9	0.161 (0.008)	–1.1
19	4,232 (105)	–15.3	0.764 (0.012)	12.5	0.352 (0.011)	19.1	0.200 (0.009)	23.0
20	4,581 (138)	–8.3	0.728 (0.016)	7.1	0.323 (0.013)	9.4	0.180 (0.010)	10.4
21	4,478 (146)	–10.4	0.741 (0.016)	9.0	0.336 (0.014)	13.7	0.190 (0.011)	16.4

Note: Standard errors, in parentheses, are calculated by bootstrapping with 300 replications, taking complex sample design into account.

Table 8.11 Means, standard errors, and percentage change of simulated consumption and poverty indexes: Urban areas using consumption per capita and region-specific food bundles

	Consumption		P_0		P_1		P_2	
Simulation number	Mean (SE)	Percent change	Mean (SE)	Percent change	Mean (SE)	Percent change	Mean (SE)	Percent change
Base	6,658		0.581		0.263		0.151	
	(397)		(0.027)		(0.019)		(0.014)	
1	6,720	0.9	0.576	−0.9	0.258	−1.7	0.148	−2.4
	(396)		(0.027)		(0.019)		(0.013)	
2	7,319	9.9	0.523	−10.1	0.217	−17.4	0.118	−22.3
	(413)		(0.028)		(0.018)		(0.012)	
3	7,630	14.6	0.503	−13.5	0.208	−20.8	0.113	−25.5
	(404)		(0.027)		(0.017)		(0.012)	
4	8,648	29.9	0.425	−26.8	0.161	−38.8	0.082	−46.0
	(554)		(0.034)		(0.019)		(0.012)	
5	8,010	20.3	0.471	−19.0	0.187	−29.0	0.098	−35.3
	(451)		(0.029)		(0.017)		(0.011)	
6	6,676	0.3	0.580	−0.3	0.262	−0.4	0.150	−0.5
	(397)		(0.027)		(0.019)		(0.014)	
7	6,678	0.3	0.580	−0.3	0.261	−0.4	0.150	−0.5
	(397)		(0.027)		(0.019)		(0.014)	
8	6,808	2.3	0.569	−2.2	0.253	−3.6	0.144	−4.6
	(416)		(0.029)		(0.020)		(0.014)	
9	6,875	3.3	0.563	−3.2	0.249	−5.4	0.141	−6.8
	(430)		(0.031)		(0.021)		(0.015)	
10	6,930	4.1	0.559	−3.9	0.246	−6.5	0.139	−8.2
	(449)		(0.032)		(0.022)		(0.016)	
11	n.a.	n.a.	n.a.	n.a.	n.a.	n.a.	n.a.	n.a.
12	n.a.	n.a.	n.a.	n.a.	n.a.	n.a.	n.a.	n.a.
13	n.a.	n.a.	n.a.	n.a.	n.a.	n.a.	n.a.	n.a.
14	n.a.	n.a.	n.a.	n.a.	n.a.	n.a.	n.a.	n.a.
15	6,707	0.7	0.579	−0.4	0.261	−0.6	0.150	−0.6
	(403)		(0.027)		(0.019)		(0.014)	
16	6,693	0.5	0.580	−0.3	0.262	−0.4	0.150	−0.5
	(400)		(0.027)		(0.019)		(0.014)	
17	6,753	1.4	0.574	−1.3	0.257	−2.0	0.148	−2.4
	(401)		(0.028)		(0.019)		(0.014)	
18	n.a.	n.a.	n.a.	n.a.	n.a.	n.a.	n.a.	n.a.
19	5,684	−14.6	0.651	12.0	0.310	17.9	0.184	21.9
	(341)		(0.027)		(0.021)		(0.016)	
20	6,110	−8.2	0.628	8.0	0.302	14.8	0.181	19.8
	(418)		(0.030)		(0.023)		(0.018)	
21	6,071	−8.8	0.631	8.5	0.306	16.6	0.186	22.8
	(424)		(0.030)		(0.023)		(0.018)	

Notes: Standard errors, in parentheses, are calculated by bootstrapping with 300 replications, taking complex sample design into account. Simulations 11–14 and 18 only pertain to rural areas; n.a. indicates "not applicable."

Table 8.12 Means, standard errors, and percentage change of simulated consumption and poverty indexes: Rural areas using consumption per AEU and region-specific food bundles

	Consumption		P_0		P_1		P_2	
Simulation number	Mean (SE)	Percent change	Mean (SE)	Percent change	Mean (SE)	Percent change	Mean (SE)	Percent change
Base	6,041 (147)		0.744 (0.013)		0.338 (0.011)		0.192 (0.009)	
1	6,296 (156)	4.2	0.723 (0.013)	−2.8	0.321 (0.011)	−5.2	0.179 (0.008)	−6.8
2	6,530 (175)	8.1	0.703 (0.015)	−5.5	0.304 (0.012)	−10.1	0.167 (0.009)	−13.1
3	6,908 (263)	14.3	0.672 (0.022)	−9.6	0.284 (0.016)	−16.1	0.153 (0.011)	−20.2
4	7,756 (451)	28.4	0.602 (0.036)	−19.0	0.236 (0.022)	−30.1	0.122 (0.014)	−36.5
5	7,424 (302)	22.9	0.630 (0.024)	−15.3	0.256 (0.016)	−24.4	0.134 (0.011)	−29.9
6	6,068 (148)	0.4	0.741 (0.013)	−0.3	0.336 (0.011)	−0.5	0.191 (0.009)	−0.6
7	6,064 (148)	0.4	0.742 (0.013)	−0.3	0.337 (0.011)	−0.4	0.191 (0.009)	−0.5
8	6,154 (181)	1.9	0.734 (0.015)	−1.3	0.332 (0.012)	−1.9	0.187 (0.009)	−2.3
9	6,266 (236)	3.7	0.725 (0.020)	−2.6	0.324 (0.015)	−4.2	0.182 (0.011)	−5.1
10	6,363 (290)	5.3	0.717 (0.025)	−3.6	0.317 (0.019)	−6.3	0.176 (0.014)	−8.0
11	6,043 (147)	0.0	0.743 (0.013)	0.0	0.338 (0.011)	0.0	0.192 (0.009)	0.0
12	6,091 (148)	0.8	0.739 (0.013)	−0.6	0.335 (0.011)	−0.9	0.190 (0.009)	−1.1
13	6,046 (147)	0.1	0.743 (0.013)	0.0	0.338 (0.011)	−0.1	0.192 (0.009)	−0.1
14	6,222 (266)	3.0	0.729 (0.023)	−2.0	0.326 (0.019)	−3.6	0.183 (0.014)	−4.6
15	6,125 (152)	1.4	0.738 (0.013)	−0.8	0.333 (0.011)	−1.4	0.188 (0.009)	−1.8
16	6,068 (148)	0.5	0.742 (0.013)	−0.2	0.337 (0.011)	−0.3	0.191 (0.009)	−0.4
17	6,102 (150)	1.0	0.739 (0.013)	−0.7	0.334 (0.011)	−1.2	0.189 (0.009)	−1.6
18	6,081 (150)	0.7	0.740 (0.013)	−0.5	0.336 (0.011)	−0.8	0.190 (0.009)	−1.0
19	5,480 (136)	−9.3	0.793 (0.012)	6.7	0.372 (0.011)	10.0	0.214 (0.009)	11.7
20	5,398 (157)	−10.6	0.803 (0.013)	8.0	0.383 (0.013)	13.1	0.222 (0.010)	16.0
21	5,305 (170)	−12.2	0.811 (0.013)	9.0	0.393 (0.014)	16.1	0.231 (0.012)	20.4

Note: Standard errors, in parentheses, are calculated by bootstrapping with 300 replications, taking complex sample design into account.

Table 8.13 Means, standard errors, and percentage change of simulated consumption and poverty indexes: Urban areas using consumption per AEU and region-specific food bundles

	Consumption		P_0		P_1		P_2	
Simulation number	Mean (SE)	Percent change	Mean (SE)	Percent change	Mean (SE)	Percent change	Mean (SE)	Percent change
Base	7,993		0.637		0.296		0.173	
	(458)		(0.026)		(0.020)		(0.015)	
1	8,069	1.0	0.632	–0.8	0.291	–1.6	0.169	–2.3
	(458)		(0.026)		(0.020)		(0.015)	
2	8,815	10.3	0.580	–8.9	0.248	–16.3	0.136	–21.2
	(482)		(0.028)		(0.019)		(0.014)	
3	9,175	14.8	0.561	–12.1	0.239	–19.4	0.131	–24.1
	(467)		(0.026)		(0.018)		(0.013)	
4	10,371	29.8	0.486	–23.8	0.190	–35.9	0.098	–43.1
	(656)		(0.035)		(0.020)		(0.013)	
5	9,610	20.2	0.531	–16.6	0.218	–26.4	0.117	–32.5
	(528)		(0.029)		(0.018)		(0.012)	
6	8,014	0.3	0.636	–0.2	0.295	–0.4	0.172	–0.4
	(458)		(0.026)		(0.020)		(0.015)	
7	8,017	0.3	0.636	–0.3	0.295	–0.4	0.172	–0.5
	(458)		(0.026)		(0.020)		(0.015)	
8	8,175	2.3	0.625	–1.9	0.286	–3.4	0.166	–4.3
	(484)		(0.028)		(0.021)		(0.016)	
9	8,257	3.3	0.620	–2.8	0.281	–5.0	0.162	–6.4
	(503)		(0.030)		(0.022)		(0.017)	
10	8,324	4.1	0.616	–3.4	0.278	–6.0	0.160	–7.8
	(526)		(0.031)		(0.023)		(0.017)	
11	n.a.	n.a.	n.a.	n.a.	n.a.	n.a.	n.a.	n.a.
12	n.a.	n.a.	n.a.	n.a.	n.a.	n.a.	n.a.	n.a.
13	n.a.	n.a.	n.a.	n.a.	n.a.	n.a.	n.a.	n.a.
14	n.a.	n.a.	n.a.	n.a.	n.a.	n.a.	n.a.	n.a.
15	8,051	0.7	0.635	–0.4	0.294	–0.6	0.172	–0.6
	(466)		(0.026)		(0.020)		(0.015)	
16	8,035	0.5	0.636	–0.2	0.295	–0.4	0.172	–0.5
	(462)		(0.026)		(0.020)		(0.015)	
17	8,106	1.4	0.630	–1.1	0.291	–1.8	0.169	–2.3
	(464)		(0.027)		(0.020)		(0.015)	
18	n.a.	n.a.	n.a.	n.a.	n.a.	n.a.	n.a.	n.a.
19	7,265	–9.1	0.679	6.5	0.325	9.8	0.193	11.8
	(420)		(0.026)		(0.021)		(0.016)	
20	7,175	–10.2	0.692	8.5	0.346	16.8	0.213	22.9
	(475)		(0.027)		(0.024)		(0.019)	
21	7,173	–10.3	0.691	8.4	0.348	17.5	0.216	24.6
	(487)		(0.028)		(0.024)		(0.019)	

Note: Standard errors, in parentheses, are calculated by bootstrapping with 300 replications, taking complex sample design into account. Simulations 11–14 and 18 only pertain to rural areas; n.a. indicates "not applicable."

Table 8.14 Means, standard errors, and percentage change of simulated consumption and poverty indexes: Rural areas using consumption per capita and single national basic needs food bundle

	Consumption		P_0		P_1		P_2	
Simulation number	Mean (SE)	Percent change	Mean (SE)	Percent change	Mean (SE)	Percent change	Mean (SE)	Percent change
Base	5,466		0.822		0.419		0.256	
	(139)		(0.010)		(0.010)		(0.009)	
1	5,700	4.3	0.806	–2.0	0.402	–4.1	0.242	–5.5
	(145)		(0.011)		(0.011)		(0.009)	
2	5,929	8.5	0.790	–3.9	0.386	–8.0	0.229	–10.6
	(169)		(0.012)		(0.012)		(0.010)	
3	5,764	5.4	0.600	–27.0	0.241	–42.5	0.126	–50.8
	(223)		(0.023)		(0.015)		(0.010)	
4	6,960	27.3	0.715	–13.0	0.321	–23.5	0.180	–29.8
	(419)		(0.031)		(0.024)		(0.017)	
5	6,721	23.0	0.732	–10.9	0.336	–19.8	0.192	–25.2
	(284)		(0.021)		(0.017)		(0.012)	
6	5,494	0.5	0.820	–0.2	0.417	–0.5	0.255	–0.6
	(139)		(0.010)		(0.010)		(0.009)	
7	5,491	0.4	0.820	–0.2	0.418	–0.4	0.255	–0.5
	(140)		(0.010)		(0.010)		(0.009)	
8	5,569	1.9	0.814	–0.9	0.413	–1.6	0.251	–1.9
	(167)		(0.012)		(0.012)		(0.010)	
9	5,668	3.7	0.807	–1.8	0.405	–3.3	0.245	–4.2
	(214)		(0.016)		(0.015)		(0.012)	
10	5,753	5.2	0.802	–2.4	0.399	–4.9	0.240	–6.5
	(260)		(0.019)		(0.019)		(0.015)	
11	5,468	0.03	0.822	–0.02	0.419	–0.03	0.256	–0.04
	(139)		(0.010)		(0.010)		(0.009)	
12	5,510	0.8	0.819	–0.4	0.416	–0.7	0.254	–0.9
	(146)		(0.010)		(0.010)		(0.009)	
13	5,471	0.1	0.822	0.0	0.419	–0.1	0.256	–0.1
	(139)		(0.010)		(0.010)		(0.009)	
14	5,636	3.1	0.810	–1.4	0.407	–2.9	0.246	–3.9
	(242)		(0.017)		(0.018)		(0.015)	
15	5,544	1.4	0.817	–0.6	0.415	–1.1	0.252	–1.5
	(144)		(0.010)		(0.011)		(0.009)	
16	5,492	0.5	0.821	–0.1	0.418	–0.3	0.255	–0.4
	(140)		(0.010)		(0.010)		(0.009)	
17	5,522	1.0	0.818	–0.5	0.415	–1.0	0.253	–1.3
	(141)		(0.010)		(0.010)		(0.009)	
18	5,504	0.7	0.819	–0.3	0.417	–0.7	0.254	–0.9
	(142)		(0.010)		(0.011)		(0.009)	
19	4,631	–15.3	0.884	7.6	0.480	14.5	0.304	18.6
	(115)		(0.008)		(0.010)		(0.010)	
20	5,011	–8.3	0.859	4.5	0.451	7.6	0.280	9.1
	(154)		(0.011)		(0.013)		(0.011)	
21	4,894	–10.5	0.867	5.5	0.463	10.4	0.290	13.2
	(159)		(0.010)		(0.013)		(0.012)	

Note: Standard errors, in parentheses, are calculated by bootstrapping with 300 replications, taking complex sample design into account.

Table 8.15 Means, standard errors, and percentage change of simulated consumption and poverty indexes: Urban areas using consumption per capita and single national basic needs food bundle

	Consumption		P_0		P_1		P_2	
Simulation number	Mean (SE)	Percent change	Mean (SE)	Percent change	Mean (SE)	Percent change	Mean (SE)	Percent change
Base	4,798		0.658		0.322		0.195	
	(229)		(0.028)		(0.021)		(0.016)	
1	4,852	1.1	0.654	–0.7	0.317	–1.4	0.191	–2.0
	(240)		(0.028)		(0.021)		(0.016)	
2	5,360	11.7	0.608	–7.7	0.275	–14.4	0.158	–19.0
	(286)		(0.029)		(0.020)		(0.015)	
3	5,559	15.9	0.587	–10.8	0.264	–17.8	0.152	–22.2
	(249)		(0.028)		(0.019)		(0.014)	
4	6,376	32.9	0.516	–21.7	0.214	–33.6	0.116	–40.7
	(386)		(0.037)		(0.023)		(0.015)	
5	5,887	22.7	0.559	–15.0	0.242	–24.7	0.135	–30.8
	(297)		(0.031)		(0.020)		(0.014)	
6	4,814	0.3	0.657	–0.2	0.320	–0.3	0.194	–0.4
	(229)		(0.028)		(0.021)		(0.016)	
7	4,816	0.4	0.657	–0.2	0.320	–0.4	0.194	–0.5
	(229)		(0.028)		(0.021)		(0.016)	
8	4,930	2.8	0.647	–1.7	0.312	–3.0	0.188	–3.8
	(255)		(0.030)		(0.023)		(0.017)	
9	4,990	4.0	0.642	–2.5	0.307	–4.4	0.184	–5.7
	(275)		(0.031)		(0.024)		(0.018)	
10	5,037	5.0	0.638	–3.1	0.304	–5.4	0.182	–6.9
	(298)		(0.033)		(0.025)		(0.019)	
11	n.a.	n.a.	n.a.	n.a.	n.a.	n.a.	n.a.	n.a.
12	n.a.	n.a.	n.a.	n.a.	n.a.	n.a.	n.a.	n.a.
13	n.a.	n.a.	n.a.	n.a.	n.a.	n.a.	n.a.	n.a.
14	n.a.	n.a.	n.a.	n.a.	n.a.	n.a.	n.a.	n.a.
15	4,839	0.9	0.656	–0.4	0.320	–0.5	0.194	–0.6
	(239)		(0.028)		(0.022)		(0.016)	
16	4,827	0.6	0.657	–0.2	0.320	–0.3	0.194	–0.4
	(235)		(0.028)		(0.021)		(0.016)	
17	4,878	1.7	0.652	–1.0	0.316	–1.7	0.191	–2.1
	(241)		(0.029)		(0.022)		(0.017)	
18	n.a.	n.a.	n.a.	n.a.	n.a.	n.a.	n.a.	n.a.
19	4,087	–14.8	0.722	9.7	0.371	15.4	0.232	19.1
	(199)		(0.026)		(0.023)		(0.018)	
20	4,412	–8.1	0.699	6.1	0.361	12.2	0.228	16.7
	(298)		(0.029)		(0.025)		(0.020)	
21	4,343	–9.5	0.701	6.4	0.365	13.4	0.232	18.8
	(284)		(0.029)		(0.025)		(0.020)	

Notes: Standard errors, in parentheses, are calculated by bootstrapping with 300 replications, taking complex sample design into account. Simulations 11–14 and 18 only pertain to rural areas; n.a. indicates "not applicable."

and SB. Not only are the base case mean consumption values different, so are all of the poverty indexes. This is because the change in the dependent variable also requires a change in the poverty line construction, and there is no guarantee that the changes in consumption and the poverty line will move in parallel. Therefore, our sensitivity analysis depends primarily on comparing the percentage changes in mean consumption and the poverty indexes across the three alternative methods. These percentage changes are also shown in Tables 8.10–8.15.

First, when mean consumption values are compared, one is struck by how the percentage changes for a given simulation are almost identical across all three methods (that is, comparing rural with rural and urban with urban). The main exception to this pattern is the demographic change simulations. As would be expected, the negative impact of an additional child is smaller when normalizing per AEU instead of per capita. Note, however, that the impact is still very negative, with a reduction in consumption per AEU of 9 percent. For additional adults, the AEU scaling shows a greater negative impact than either of the per capita approaches.

Turning to the poverty measures, we see that there is greater variation in outcomes across methods, with some clear patterns. For example, the MB method consistently shows larger percentage reductions in poverty than either the AEU or SB method. The comparison between AEU and SB is closer, with AEU tending to show higher percentage changes in poverty than SB. Once again, however, it bears mentioning that although these differences are evident, there are no cases where different methods have opposite signs on the change in poverty, and the magnitude of the differences is usually small.

Does this mean that the MB method employed here produces biased estimates of changes in poverty? Probably not. The explanation for close matches on mean consumption but systematic differences in poverty measures can be easily explained by the position of the poverty line relative to the income distribution. Figure 8.1 shows the distribution of log consumption per capita from the IAF data, as measured by the MB method. Note that per capita consumption is approximately lognormal. The three vertical lines are the three poverty lines corresponding to the three methods being compared, with the leftmost line being the MB method, the middle being the AEU method, and the line furthest to the right the SB method. The proportion of the area under the curve that is to the left of the poverty line gives the headcount index for that combination of income distribution and poverty line. The order of the lines is consistent with the results shown for the base simulation for each of the three methods: Tables 8.10–8.15 show that in the base simulation, measured poverty increases as one moves from MB to AEU to SB.[57]

Poverty reduction implies shifting the income distribution to the right, with the absolute poverty line remaining fixed in real terms. It may be a uniform, parallel shift of the curve, but more often different parts of the curve shift at different rates. The important point for the present discussion, however, is that the percentage change in poverty is greatest for MB and least for SB because of their positions relative to the income distribution. The MB line is closest to the mass of the distribution, so that for an

[57]To simplify the presentation, Figure 8.1 shows only a single distribution of real consumption. In fact, each of the alternatives is associated not only with a distinct set of poverty lines, but also with slightly different distributions of real consumption. The argument presented here still applies if the consumption distribution and poverty lines for each of the three methods are plotted separately.

Figure 8.1 Income distribution and three alternative poverty lines

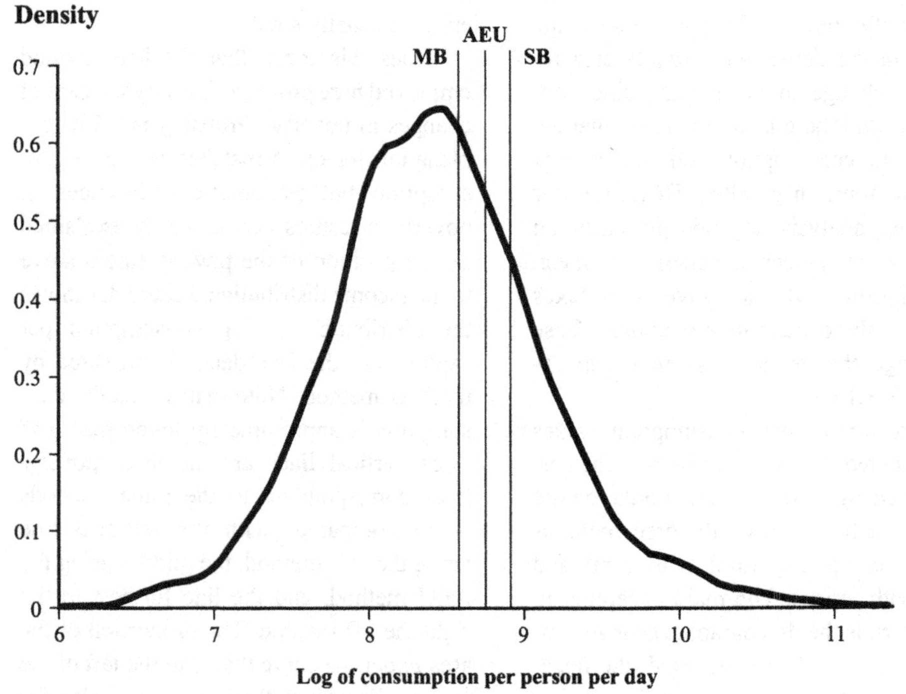

Source: Mozambique National Household Survey of Living Conditions, 1996–97.

equivalent shift to the right, a higher proportion of the population will pass the MB line than will pass either of the other two poverty lines. The same is true for increases in poverty (leftward shifts of the distribution); because MB is closer to the mode of the distribution, it will show larger increases in poverty than the other methods. Analogous arguments apply to the poverty gap and squared poverty gap measures.

It should be noted that not all of these patterns are universal. For example, in a country where most of the population is above the poverty lines, the lines will lie to the left of the mode of the distribution, and it will be the highest, rather than the lowest, poverty line that will "catch" the largest share of the population moving across the poverty line. Likewise, the MB method will not always produce the lowest poverty measures. It is possible for the AEU approach to yield lower poverty indexes than either of the per capita approaches. However, MB will always produce lower poverty lines and lower poverty rates than SB, because the national average food consumption bundle at the heart of the SB method is not a cost minimizing bundle for any specific region (see Tarp et al. 2002b for further discussion of this issue).

Overall, we conclude that the results of the simulations are not very sensitive to the choice of method. The largest differences occur when using the AEU normalization on the demographic change simulations, but even the overall pattern of large poverty increases is maintained for each of those simulations.

CHAPTER 9

Economic Growth and Poverty Reduction

Economic growth has been widely regarded as a key pillar of the strategy for poverty reduction. This is especially obvious in Mozambique, where at the time of the IAF survey mean consumption per capita was actually below the absolute poverty line. Many of the policy simulations that we have considered clearly work through fostering economic growth, as, for instance, in the case of economic infrastructure development. Similarly, human capital development can also be considered an important ingredient of the process of economic growth. In this chapter, we abstract from the potential sources or determinants of growth and pose the question: how much potential does economic growth, whatever its source, hold for poverty reduction in Mozambique?

We first look at the recent historical experience. Based on national accounts data, it is estimated that real per capita GDP in Mozambique grew by 6.5 percent over the decade 1987–96, for a modest increase of less than 1 percent per year.[58] Even though there was no household survey with national coverage prior to the IAF 1996–97, it is possible to use the IAF data to explore what sort of poverty impact this growth could have had.[59] In particular, one can estimate what poverty levels would have been in 1987 had average living standards grown at the same rate as real GDP per capita, assuming there was no change in relative inequalities. This is equivalent to simulating a distribution-neutral growth scenario where every household's consumption increases proportionately by the same growth factor.

Table 9.1 summarizes the findings of this analysis. It shows that under the distribution-neutral assumption, the poverty reduction impact of that growth was small. Over the 10-year

Table 9.1 Implications of economic growth over the past decade for poverty reduction

Welfare measure	1987 simulated	1996–97	Percent change over the decade
Mean consumption			
(MT per person per day at 1996–97 prices)	4,963	5,286	6.5
Headcount index	0.726	0.694	–4.4
Poverty gap index	0.318	0.293	–8.0
Squared poverty gap index	0.174	0.156	–10.1

Note: MT is meticais.

[58]These estimates are based on the official GDP figures published by the INE in various issues of the Anuário Estatístico (INE 1996, 1997, 1998). In these calculations, the nominal per capita GDP was deflated by the CPI for Maputo City.

[59]Similar calculations for Bangladesh are presented in Ravallion and Sen (1996).

period, such growth would have implied a decline in the incidence of poverty of about 4.4 percent, and a decline in the depth and severity of poverty of about 8 and 10 percent, respectively.

Table 9.2 presents the potential implications of higher growth in the future, under various assumptions about the rate of economic growth and the distribution of that growth. In the first scenario, a moderate growth rate of per capita consumption of 2 percent per year is considered, with the gains of this growth distributed proportionately (implying no change in the Lorenz curve). This growth scenario generates significant gains in poverty reduction, especially as measured by the poverty gap and squared poverty gap indexes.

Next, in each of the scenarios 2, 3, and 4 in Table 9.2, a much faster consumption growth rate is assumed, 4 percent in real per capita terms with three alternative distributional assumptions. This rate of growth in private consumption is based upon the government's five-year growth projections for 1999–2003 , assuming a population growth rate of 2.4 percent per year. In Scenario 2, growth is assumed to be distribution-neutral (as in the first scenario). Faster growth relative to Scenario 1, of course, leads to

Table 9.2 Implications of future economic growth for poverty reduction

Hypothetical economic growth rate	1996–97	2003 simulated	Percent change over five years
Scenario 1: 2%/year growth in real consumption per capita, distribution-neutral			
Mean consumption (MT/person/day at 1996–97 prices)	5,286	5,836	10.4
Headcount index	0.694	0.642	–7.5
Poverty gap index	0.293	0.254	–13.4
Squared poverty gap index	0.156	0.131	–16.4
Scenario 2: 4%/year growth in real consumption per capita, distribution-neutral			
Mean consumption (MT/person/day at 1996–97 prices)	5,286	6,688	26.5
Headcount index	0.694	0.553	–20.3
Poverty gap index	0.293	0.203	–30.6
Squared poverty gap index	0.156	0.010	–36.2
Scenario 3: 4%/year growth in real consumption per capita, with growth in urban areas twice as fast as rural growth			
Mean consumption (MT/person/day at 1996–97 prices)	5,286	6,688	26.5
Headcount index	0.694	0.566	–18.4
Poverty gap index	0.293	0.209	–28.7
Squared poverty gap index	0.156	0.103	–33.9
Scenario 4: 4%/year growth in real consumption per capita, with growth for nonpoor households twice as fast as for poor households			
Mean consumption (MT/person/day at 1996–97 prices)	5,286	6,688	26.5
Headcount index	0.694	0.606	–12.6
Poverty gap index	0.293	0.232	–20.6
Squared poverty gap index	0.156	0.117	–24.9

Note: MT is meticais.

greater poverty reduction relative to Scenario 1. Such growth, if sustained from 1997 to 2003, would lead to a reduction in the national poverty headcount index of about 20 percent. Even larger percentage declines are implied for the poverty gap and squared poverty gap indexes, indicating that the remaining poor would be less poor than before.

There is evidence from experience in other countries that economic growth as rapid as that projected for Mozambique is typically not distributed equally, but tends to increase inequality.[60] Thus, Scenario 3 illustrates the effects on poverty of the same economic growth rate, with urban incomes growing twice as rapidly as rural incomes. In this scenario, poverty reduction is somewhat lower than that projected in the distribution-neutral scenario (Scenario 2), yet the reduction in all poverty measures is still substantial (Table 9.2). Finally, Scenario 4 shows the effects of economic growth on poverty reduction if the incomes of the nonpoor grow twice as fast as the incomes of the poor. Under this skewed pattern of economic growth, the reduction in poverty is less than that in Scenarios 2 and 3, yet poverty reduction is still significant, with the headcount declining by 13 percent, leaving 61 percent of the population below the poverty line by the year 2003.

These growth simulations demonstrate that economic growth can be a potent force for poverty reduction. That said, the pattern and distribution of that growth would also have an important bearing on the degree to which poverty is reduced.

[60]There is also evidence to the contrary, and this has reemerged as a contentious topic in recent years. For a sampling of the debate, see Dollar and Kraay (2001), Ravallion (2001), and subsequent articles in recent issues of *Foreign Affairs* (Dollar and Kraay 2002a and 2002b; and Galbraith 2002).

CHAPTER 10

Conclusions and Implications for Policy

The analysis presented in this report seeks to extend the understanding of poverty in Mozambique by going beyond the bivariate analysis of a typical poverty profile to examine the determinants of living standards and poverty. Before summarizing the key implications of the results for the formulation of poverty reduction policies in Mozambique, it is useful to mention some caveats to the analysis and results presented here.

As the first nationally representative household survey, the IAF survey provides a wealth of useful information on household living conditions. However, the survey data also have some significant limitations that have influenced the analysis presented in this study. A significant omission among the potential determinants of poverty is some measure of agricultural yields. This measure is omitted because of the lack of regionally disaggregated data on yields that could be integrated with data from the IAF survey. It would be useful to collect such data in future surveys both to promote better analysis of the determinants of poverty and living standards and to facilitate monitoring of poverty over time.

There also seems to be a considerable degree of measurement error for a number of variables on which data were collected in the IAF survey, including, for instance, the distance to facilities, area of *machamba*, and the quantities of output produced and sold. While a considerable amount of effort was spent in cleaning the data (including corrections made by going back to the original questionnaires), the existence of measurement errors influenced the specification choices that were made in the analytical work (for example, the need to form crude indexes of infrastructure development for the poverty determinants models). Another limitation has to do with the lack of data on fisheries as a form of livelihood. We suspect that fisheries make a potentially important contribution to living standards of households, especially in the coastal region. However, the IAF employment data report an extremely small proportion of the population engaged in fishing. While we partially control for this by way of district fixed effects, we are unable to isolate the individual effect.

These limitations suggest scope for improvement in future data collection efforts and also a need for caution against a highly literal interpretation of the results presented in this study. It is more judicious to focus on broad regularities than on the exact numbers. Furthermore, it should be emphasized that the analyses here are primarily partial equilibrium in nature. The simulated changes would undoubtedly cause changes in other variables such as wages or prices, which may either accentuate or attenuate the effects predicted by our simulation models. Reduced form regression models are not particularly good at capturing general equilibrium relationships. For example, the simulations probably overstate the impact of primary education, because at least a portion of the higher earnings of those with more education may be attributed to "credentialism" rather than higher productivity. If a large portion of the population completed primary education, it is unlikely that it would provide the same premium that it does at present. Tarp et al. (2002a) provide a general equilibrium treatment of economic development issues in Mozambique, the trade-off being that they cannot provide as much detail on the distributional effects as is provided here.

Drawing upon the analysis presented here, we may identify five principal elements of a prospective poverty reduction strategy for Mozambique. These include (1) increased investment in education, (2) sustained economic growth, (3) measures to raise agricultural productivity, (4) improved rural infrastructure, and (5) reduction of the birthrate and dependency load within households. Each of these elements is elaborated upon in turn.

One of the key messages of the analysis is that it is important to invest in education. As a basic nonincome dimension of well-being, education is important in its own right. From this perspective, high priority should be given to addressing the gender, urban-rural, and regional disparities in educational attainment that presently exist. The gaps in education between males and females and between urban and rural dwellers are large and significant. Similarly, provinces such as Niassa, Cabo Delgado, Nampula, Zambézia, and Sofala have lagged critically behind in building their human capital resource base. The process of raising the overall educational standards in the country can indeed take the form of addressing these imbalances.

Education also has instrumental value; the analysis shows that education is a key determinant of living standards and improvements in education are an important means of poverty reduction. Completing primary education, in particular, is associated with large gains in poverty reduction, although the poverty-reducing impact of higher literacy rates alone are also significant. Overall, it seems clear that investing in education should be a key element of the poverty reduction strategy for Mozambique.

The analysis also points to the importance of economic growth for poverty reduction. Not much by way of poverty alleviation could have been expected over the preceding two decades of economic decline or stagnation at best. During 1987–96, real per capita GDP grew at only about 0.6 percent per year. However, economic growth does hold the promise of significant poverty reduction in the future. For instance, a sustained annual growth rate in consumption of 4 percent in real per capita terms over the last five years has had the potential of reducing the incidence of poverty by as much as 20 percent (14 percentage points), although the actual poverty reduction would also depend critically upon the distribution of growth.

The sectoral pattern of growth is important. At the current productivity levels and structure of the economy, employment in the industrial and services sectors is associated with higher living standards. However, promoting growth and employment in those sectors typically also depends on increases in agricultural productivity. The relatively high levels of poverty in the agricultural sector reflect the currently low levels of productivity in that sector. The results indicate that increasing the size of landholdings for small landholders is unlikely to reduce poverty significantly unless productivity-enhancing investments are made in the promotion of improved agricultural inputs, such as improved seed, fertilizers, and mechanization. This is not entirely surprising in a setting where the availability of land does not appear to be a binding constraint.

An important role is also identified for improved economic infrastructure in rural areas. Wider provision of roads, markets, banks, and extension and communication services to Mozambican villages can go a long way in alleviating poverty in the country.

The results also suggest that measures to reduce the dependency load within households will help reduce poverty. Apart from the direct effect of reducing the number of children supported by an adult of working age, the beneficial effects of lower fecundity on women's health, labor force participation, and productivity could also help reduce poverty. Drawing upon the experience of other countries, the importance of women's education in this context cannot be overemphasized.

Finally, it should be reiterated that while this analysis has helped identify some key directions for a poverty reduction policy, there is a need to extend and refine this analysis, including more disaggregated analyses at the regional and provincial levels, as well as incorporating supplementary information from other recent data sources, such as the national agricultural survey, the demographic and health survey, and the national census, and available geographic information systems. Furthermore, setting priorities among these policy interventions will require an assessment of the cost-effectiveness of alternative policies.

APPENDIX 1

Constructing Aggregate Household Consumption as a Welfare Measure

This study uses a comprehensive measure of consumption, drawing from several modules of the household survey. The approach used follows closely that described by Deaton and Zaidi (1999) and Deaton and Grosh (2000). It includes expenditures and autoconsumption of food and nonfood items, as well as imputed use values for owner-occupied housing and household durable goods. The only significant omission from the consumption measure is consumption of commodities supplied by the public sector free of charge or the subsidized element in such commodities. For example, an all-weather road, or a public market, or a public water tap, presumably enhances the well-being of the people who use those facilities. However, the IAF data do not permit quantification of those benefits, and they are therefore not included in the consumption measure.[61]

Food Consumption

In the IAF, information on household food acquisition was recorded in the daily household expenses questionnaire. As described in Chapter 3, households were visited three times over a seven-day period and asked what foods the household had acquired and through what means, including purchases, own production, and transfers received. On each visit the household was asked what food was acquired that day, as well as the preceding two days (on the second and third visits), so that food acquisition information was recorded separately for each of seven days. The most common food items were precoded on the questionnaire, but the questions were open-ended, so that the household could include any food items that were acquired.

For each food item recorded, the interviewer solicited information about the unit of measure for the item (for example, kilograms, liters, cans, cups, and so forth), the number of those units acquired, and the amount spent for the food. If the item was received in a noncash transfer or was home-produced, then the respondent provided an estimate of the value of the food. The household was also asked how many days they expected the food would last in the household and from where they acquired the food (shop, market, informal market, own-production, or other). For example, a household might respond that the previous day they had spent 60,000 meticais on two *latas* (cans) of maize grain from a local market and they expected it to last for eight days.

[61]This, however, is not unique to the Mozambique survey. It is rarely possible to integrate the consumption of public goods into an aggregate measure of consumption.

The daily household expenses questionnaire was designed to collect food acquisition information for a seven-day period. However, consumption of individual products acquired and recorded on the questionnaire may span more or less than one week. All food consumption was normalized to reflect average consumption for a one-week period, calculated as follows. The expenditure (or, more generally, the value), physical quantity consumed, and number of days the food would last were summed for each product. If the total estimated number of days the food would last was less than or equal to seven, then it was assumed that the survey captured a typical week's worth of that food item for that household. The sums of the item's value and physical quantity were then divided by seven to arrive at estimated daily consumption values for that food item. If the estimated number of days the food would last exceeded seven days (for example, a bulk purchase of maize grain or flour, or three separate purchases of a three-day supply), the total quantity and expenditure recorded were divided by the estimated number of days the food would last to arrive at an estimate of the average daily consumption of that food item. The estimates of daily food consumption for each item were then aggregated to the household level to obtain an estimate of the total value of household food consumption per day.

Nonfood Consumption

Nonfood consumption is the sum of several nonfood consumption components, including both direct expenditures and imputed use values. The details of the construction of these components are described below.

Monthly and Three-Month Nonfood Consumption

Two sections of the IAF questionnaire were devoted exclusively to the collection of information about nonfood expenditures; the two sections differ only by recall period and the list of items covered. The monthly nonfood expenditure section of the questionnaire asked primarily about common consumable nonfood items acquired by the household during the preceding month, including items such as cooking fuel, medicines, soap, and other items. The three-month nonfood expenditures questionnaire had a three-month recall period; it is intended to capture less frequent purchases, such as clothing and footwear, household durables, and other items that are generally more expensive than those recorded in the monthly nonfood expenditures questionnaire. Each of these sections of the questionnaire also asked about the quantity of the item purchased, the value of the item, and the location where the item was purchased. For most items, converting to household daily consumption values was simply a matter of dividing the values from the monthly questionnaire by 30.417 (365 days/12 months), and those in the three-month questionnaire by 91.25 (365 days/4 quarters). However, for certain expensive, infrequently purchased durable goods, a different approach was used. In these cases, a use value for the item was imputed for all households possessing that item, as recorded in the household assets section of the IAF questionnaire, whether it had been purchased during the survey recall period or not. This is described in detail below.

Housing and Imputed Rent

A comprehensive measure of consumption as a measure of welfare should include a value for the use of housing. When a household pays rent for its dwelling, this is measured by the actual rent paid. For owner-occupied houses, too, data on self-imputed rents are available for some households in the form of responses to the question, "If you had to rent your house, how much would you charge per month?" Thus, we have a measure of actual rent for tenants and a measure of self-estimated rental value for owner-occupants. These data on actual or self-imputed rents are used whenever available. However, for 6,986 households, no such information is available. For these households, we estimate an imputed rent, or the use value of the housing, as a function of a number of dwelling characteristics—information that was collected for almost all households. A hedonic rental model is estimated using the 1,264 households who reported actual or self-estimated rents. Rents are then imputed for the remaining 6,986 households, using their dwelling characteristics and the estimated parameters from the rental model.

We use data on both actual and self-imputed rents in our rent determination model. The following model was estimated.

$$\ln R_i = \alpha + \beta' (Province{*}Urban)_i + \gamma (Tenant)_i + \delta' X_i + \varepsilon_i$$

where

R_i = monthly rent (actual or self-imputed) for household i;

$(Province{*}\ Urban)_i$ = a set of dummy variables for interactions between province and rural or urban zone residence;

$Tenant_i$ = a dummy variable with a value of 1 if the rent observation is reported by a tenant and 0 if self-imputed by the owner;

X_i = a vector of dwelling characteristics, including number of rooms, categorical variables identifying the type of dwelling (house, apartment, or hut), the type of walls, roof, floor, toilet, source of water, age of the dwelling, length of stay in the dwelling, mode of acquisition of dwelling, type of illumination, and the type of cooking fuel used.

The dummy variable for *Tenant* turned out to be collinear with the other model variables and was dropped. We also tried several alternative specifications, including interacting the *Tenant* dummy variable with dwelling characteristics; interaction terms for dwelling type and the set of dummy variables for province and rural or urban area; and running separate regressions by type of dwelling: one for *vivendas* (houses) and flats and the other for *palhotas* (huts) and other dwellings. However, none of these specifications improved the model's fit significantly.

Our preferred estimates of the model parameters are reported in Table A1.1. The estimated parameters were used to impute rent for cases where actual or self-imputed rent was not available.

Use Value of Durable Goods

The consumption of durable goods augments household welfare and hence should be included as a component of aggregate household consumption. However, the consumption of durable goods is distinct from their purchase or acquisition because, typically, durable goods are purchased or acquired infrequently and consumed over long periods of time. This is in contrast to nondurable or single-use goods whose consumption is usually realized over a relatively short period of time. The value of durable goods purchased over a certain time period can therefore be a poor measure of the value of their consumption over that period.

The use value of durable goods has two components: the depreciation of the durable good over the period of consumption considered, and the opportunity cost of resources locked in the durable good over that period of consumption. Thus, the value of consumption of durable good j for household i can be estimated as

$Use\ value_{ij} = Current\ value_{ij}\ (r + d_j) / (1 - d_j)$,

Table A1.1 A hedonic model for dwelling rentals (dependent variable: log monthly rental)

Variable	Parameter estimate	t-ratio
Province-zone dummy variables		
Niassa, rural	0.2177	0.219
Cabo Delgado, urban	–0.8069	–0.961
Cabo Delgado, rural	–0.6334	–0.744
Nampula, urban	–0.6364	–0.777
Nampula, rural	–1.6189	–1.744
Zambézia, urban	–0.6126	–0.738
Zambézia, rural	0.2602	0.255
Tete, urban	–0.6668	–0.809
Tete, rural	–0.9496	–1.039
Manica, urban	–0.3465	–0.425
Manica, rural	–0.5468	–0.644
Sofala, urban	–0.0734	–0.09
Sofala, rural	–0.0592	–0.066
Inhambane, urban	–0.0330	–0.04
Inhambane, rural	–0.3272	–0.403
Gaza, urban	0.0315	0.034
Gaza, rural	–0.6533	–0.79
Maputo Province, urban	–0.2042	–0.252
Maputo Province, rural	–0.3884	–0.475
Maputo City, urban	0.0058	0.007
Number of rooms		
Number of rooms in dwelling	0.1405	5.502
Missing data (dummy)	1.7456	1.381
Type of habitation dummy variables		
Flat or apartment	–0.1355	–0.937
Hut (palhota) or cabana	–0.0415	–0.14
Other	–0.4036	–2.113
Type of walls dummy variables		
Wood or metal	–0.4419	–2.297
Adobe	–0.4227	–1.337
Reeds or sticks	–0.3173	–1.141
Reeds or sticks with mud plaster	–0.5155	–1.738
Other	–0.3803	–0.914
Type of roof dummy variables		
Tile	–0.0744	–0.352
Composite	–0.2778	–1.73
Zinc	–0.1266	–0.954
Thatch	–0.3766	–1.542
Other	–0.0964	–0.437
Type of floor dummy variables		
Marble	–0.2061	–0.773
Granulite	–0.1976	–0.322
Cement or concrete	0.1043	0.699
Brick	0.5395	1.118
Adobe	–0.2763	–1.138
None (earthen)	–0.0740	–0.323
Other	0.7626	2.324
If any room used exclusively for work (dummy variables)		
No	0.0906	0.605
Missing data	–0.0717	–0.198

(continued)

Table A1.1—Continued

Variable	Parameter estimate	t-ratio
Age of dwelling dummy variables		
1 to 3 years	0.2541	0.888
4 to 5 years	0.0929	0.324
5 to 10 years	0.2908	1.052
More than 10 years	0.2660	1.005
Missing data	0.3093	0.483
Length of stay dummy variables		
1 to 3 years	–0.3417	–1.528
4 to 5 years	–0.1328	–0.578
5 to 10 years	–0.4622	–2.116
More than 10 years	–0.2913	–1.436
Missing data	–0.8119	–0.714
Mode of acquisition dummy variables		
Rented (not from APIE/Coop)	2.1516	12.352
Own home, fully paid	3.0307	25.326
Own home, still paying for it	2.4742	12.509
Squatting	2.6088	10.706
Ceded by the state or others	1.2370	4.609
Other	0.6142	0.863
Source of water dummy variables		
Piped water in yard	–0.1991	–1.645
Public tap	–0.3903	–2.595
Private well	–0.3534	–1.964
Public well	–0.3623	–2.194
River or lake	–0.3010	–1.232
Other	–0.3587	–2.285
If dwelling has a toilet dummy variables		
No	0.0614	0.086
Missing data	0.0532	0.069
If dwelling has a latrine dummy variables		
No	0.1435	1.333
Missing data	0.3132	0.442
Type of illumination dummy variables		
Oil lamp	–0.3010	–3.083
Candle	–0.3320	–1.467
Wood	–0.6080	–2.943
Other	–0.5968	–2.200
No lighting	–0.0705	–0.131
Type of cooking fuel dummy variables		
Gas	–0.1769	–1.128
Charcoal	–0.1510	–1.211
Wood	–0.3248	–2.178
Other	–0.0972	–0.293
Do not cook	–0.5376	–0.478
Constant	9.3043	10.833
R^2	0.5947	
Adjusted R^2	0.5673	
Standard error of regression	1.1006	
Signif. F = .0000 F(80,1183)	21.6987	

Note: The regression uses observations on actual or owner-estimated rent reported by 1,264 households. APIE is the state housing agency.

where *Current value*$_{ij}$ is the value of good j for household i at the time of the survey, r is the rate of interest, and d_j is the rate of depreciation of good j.

The IAF questionnaire asked households about their possession of 16 durable goods. Examples of durable goods include furniture, vehicles, bicycles, and other household articles such as electric irons, fans, radios, and televisions. The survey asked about the quantity and the condition of each good (whether they were in "good" condition) but not its value. It was therefore necessary to estimate the value of these durable goods at the time of the survey (February 1996 to April 1997). To derive this value, a modest market survey was conducted in Maputo City that collected information on the market prices of goods prevailing in September 1996, the midpoint of the survey.

The primary source for the price data was the Maputo informal market for used goods. For cases where the price of a used good was not obtainable, the value of new goods in the formal market was used. For cases where the value of goods in September 1996 was difficult to find, the current value at the time of the Maputo market survey, October 1997, was used. Prices of new goods were converted to used goods equivalents, assuming that the value of a used good was two-thirds the value of a comparable new good.

Prices current at the time of the market survey—October 1997—were deflated to the midpoint of the survey period (September 1996) using the durable goods component of the consumer price index (CPI) compiled by the National Institute of Statistics (INE 1997). A deflator of 0.89 was used to convert October 1997 prices to September 1996 prices. The resulting values are presented in Table A1.2.

Recall that the questionnaire identified the total quantity of a particular durable good that the household possessed and the quantity in good condition, with the rest presumably in "bad" condition. In computing the current value of durable goods, the value of goods in bad condition was assumed to be half the value of those in good condition.

The next step was the estimation of depreciation rates for durable goods based on their estimated remaining life span, keeping in mind that households report possession of durable goods they have already been using over a period of time. The estimated life spans were based on informal consultations with several members of the staff at the Department of Population and Social Development in the Ministry of Planning and Finance and are shown in the last column of Table A1.2.[62] A straight-line depreciation method was used to compute a monthly depreciation rate for each good, that is, the monthly depreciation rate is the inverse of the lifetime of the durable good in months.

Finally, to estimate the opportunity cost component, we used the interest rate on bank deposits. For our purposes, we used the average interest rate over the duration of the household survey, as reported in the Central Bank Statistical Yearbook (Banco de Moçambique 1997).

Our estimation of the use value of durable goods involves several strong assumptions necessitated by the lack of appropriate data. However, we felt that even an approximate estimate was better than a complete omission of this component from our measure of household consumption (see Deaton and Zaidi 1999).

---

[62]In principle, we could use the depreciation rates established in the tax law and used in business. However, that was not pursued, as these rates were not believed to be representative of used durable goods at the household level.

Table A1.2 Estimated market values and life spans of durable goods

Durable good	Estimated market value of a used durable good at the time of the IAF survey (1,000 meticais)	Assumed remaining life span (in years)
Table with four chairs	2,352	15
Medium bed	358	15
Refrigerator	6,638	10
Fan	149	5
Sewing machine	3,876	25
Electrical iron	224	5
Charcoal iron	30	5
Radio	251	5
Black and white television	1,700	5
Color television	3,506	5
Air conditioner	5,665	10
Clock	72	5
Telephone	519	10
Vehicle (car or truck)	125,029	15
Motorcycle	13,892	10
Bicycle	795	10

Note: The estimated market values are for a used durable good in "good" condition. See text for further discussion of data sources and assumptions used in the calculations.

Other Nonfood Consumption

Other nonfood consumption items were drawn from various parts of the IAF questionnaire. Although the daily expenditure questionnaire was mostly used to record food expenditures, it also included purchases of fuel (firewood, charcoal, kerosene), soap, water, and local transportation (minibuses, or *chapas*). Additional observations on energy and water consumption appeared in the dwelling (*vivenda*) section of the questionnaire. In cases where expenses on a particular category appeared in more than one section of the questionnaire, the data were crosschecked to avoid double counting of any consumption items. Expenditures on school fees and books were drawn from the education section of the questionnaire. Finally, there were a few types of transfers or financial transactions made by the household that were included in the measure of aggregate consumption, namely, payments made for life and health insurance and payments made to clubs or associations.

Temporal Differences in Food Prices

A potentially important issue for constructing region-specific poverty lines is seasonal (or more generally, temporal) variation in prices, especially food prices. It is commonly observed that food prices in Mozambique fluctuate substantially across seasons. Seasonal price variation need not bias the regional poverty profile if household interviews in each poverty line region were uniformly spread through the survey period. However, Table 3.2, which lists the distribution of sample households by month of interview and region, shows that this was not the case, particularly for urban areas.

Even if the temporal distribution of interviews in each poverty line region were uniform, the nonregional aspects of the poverty profile can be biased by seasonal variation in prices. For the IAF data, seasonal price variation has an additional bearing on the calculation of poverty lines because the quantities, and hence calories, consumed by households often have to be determined using data on food prices.

We examined the nature of seasonal variation in food prices using price data from the Agricultural Market Information System (Sistema de Informação do Mercado Agrícola, or SIMA) of the Ministry of Agriculture and Fisheries. We constructed a temporal food price index for the relatively poor (for this purpose, defined as households with nominal per capita consumption below the median). The price indexes were constructed separately for three regions in the country, designated as northern, central, and southern. Reporting markets for Niassa, Cabo Delgado, and Nampula provinces were included in the northern region; those for Sofala, Tete, Manica, and Zambézia provinces were included in the central region; and the southern region included markets for Gaza, Inhambane, and Maputo provinces and Maputo City. The food price index was based on nine food products: maize grain, maize flour, cassava flour, rice, sugar, cowpeas, butter beans, small groundnuts, and large groundnuts. These nine products accounted for approximately one-half of the total nominal food consumption of the relatively poor: 48 percent for the northern, 54 percent for the central, and 46 percent for the southern region. Average product prices for each region were aggregated into an index, using as weights the region-specific expenditure share of each product in total food expenditure of the relatively poor.

The pattern of the food price index is illustrated in Figure A1.1. Food prices are highest at the beginning of the survey in February 1996, drop significantly during the middle of the calendar year, and rise somewhat during the last months of 1996 and the first months of 1997. It is notable that this pattern corresponds roughly to the harvest cycle. Food prices are highest in the beginning of the calendar year, when the stocks from the preceding harvest are depleted for most households. Early harvest of green maize and other crops eases the pressure on food prices until they reach their lowest point following the harvest, which typically occurs during May, June, and July. Then prices rise again in December and January, although in this instance the prices in early 1997 were generally much lower than those for the corresponding period in 1996. Although the monthly data in Figure A1.1 illustrate the price cycles well, we chose to aggregate the price data, using four-month averages. The indexes were constructed for four subperiods spanning the duration of the IAF: subperiod 1 from February 1996 to April 1996, subperiod 2 from May 1996 to August 1996, subperiod 3 from September 1996 to December 1996, and subperiod 4 from January 1997 to April 1997. The estimated indexes are not reported here but can be found in MPF/UEM/IFPRI (1998, Table 1.5).

Overall, the results indicate significant temporal variation in food prices in all regions, with higher prices during February to April 1996 (the lean months before the annual harvest), followed by a decline and leveling off in the next two subperiods, and an increase again during January to April 1997. In view of this evidence, we deflated nominal food consumption by the seasonal food price indexes. Thus, food consumption aggregates are expressed at January–April 1997 prices. We assume that there is no temporal variation in nonfood prices. This may be an oversimplification, but given the available data, we could not replace this with a better assumption. Furthermore, considering the low level of inflation in Mozambique during the survey period and the lack of any compelling reason to expect seasonal (or any other systematic intrayear) fluctuations in prices, it is likely that any temporal adjustment to nonfood prices would be small even if sufficient data were available. Our temporally price-adjusted household total consumption is thus the sum of temporally price-adjusted food consumption plus nominal nonfood consumption.

Figure A1.1 Temporal food price variation, by region

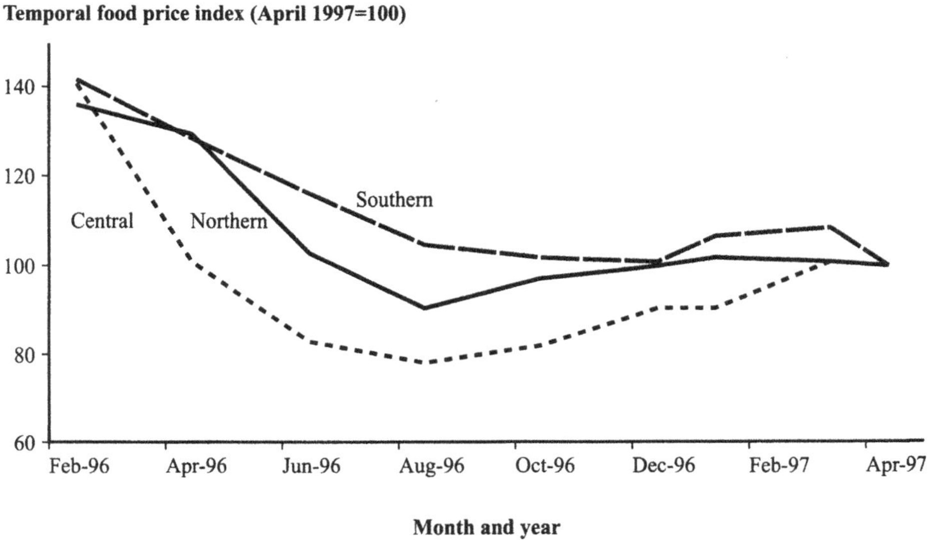

Source: Ministry of Agriculture and Fisheries, Market Price Information System 1996–97.

Composition of Household Consumption

A typical analysis of household expenditure patterns, based upon expenditure shares for functional groupings of food and nonfood commodities, is presented in the poverty profile in Chapter 2 of MPF/UEM/IFPRI (1998). However, from a methodological point of view, it is useful at this point to examine the relative magnitudes of the different components of the consumption measure used in this study. Reviewing the components of total household consumption, we note that, on average, food consumption is by far the largest component of total consumption, accounting for 62 percent of total consumption. A high food budget share such as this is typical for very low-income countries such as Mozambique. The second largest component is the estimated use value of durable goods, which accounts for 12 percent of total consumption. This is followed by nonfood items from the daily expenditure questionnaire—predominantly energy items such as firewood and charcoal—which comprise 9 percent of total consumption. Housing, either in the form of rent paid or an imputed value for housing services, is next on the list, accounting for 6 percent of total consumption. The items appearing in the three-month and monthly nonfood expenditure questionnaires are the next largest components, at 6 percent and 4 percent, respectively. The remaining components of total expenditure account for less than 1 percent of total consumption individually and only 1.5 percent collectively.

APPENDIX 2

Formulae for Simulating Poverty Measures from Regression Models of Household Consumption

As discussed in Chapter 2, a commonly used technique in poverty analysis is to estimate empirical models of household consumption (normalized in per capita or per adult equivalent terms) and then to simulate levels of poverty based on the estimated parameters. Chapter 8 describes how the headcount index as a measure of poverty could be simulated under this approach. This appendix provides additional formulae for simulating poverty measures within the Foster-Greer-Thorbecke class (in particular the poverty gap and the squared poverty gap indexes), starting from a consumption model such as the following:

$$\ln c_j = \beta' x_j + \varepsilon_j \text{ where } u_j = \varepsilon_j / \sigma \sim N(0,1)$$

where log consumption ($\ln c_j$) for household j is modeled as function of a set of relevant characteristics for the household and a normally distributed error term.

Table A2.1 gives the necessary formulae.

Table A2.1 Formulae for predictions of poverty measures from household consumption models

Consumption model	(A1) $\ln c_j = \beta' x_j + \varepsilon_j$ where $u_j = \varepsilon_j / \sigma \sim N(0,1)$
Predictions:	
Consumption for household j	(A2) $\hat{c}_j = e^{(\hat{\beta}' x_j + \hat{\sigma}^2/2)}$
Headcount index for household j	(A3) $\hat{P}_{0j} = \Phi\left\{\frac{1}{\hat{\sigma}}(\ln z - \hat{\beta}' x_j)\right\}$
Poverty gap index for household j	(A4) $\hat{P}_{1j} = \hat{\sigma} e^{(\hat{\beta}' x_j + \hat{\sigma}^2/2)} \Phi\left\{\frac{1}{\hat{\sigma}}(\ln z - \hat{\beta}' x_j) - \hat{\sigma}\right\} - \hat{\sigma} e^{2\hat{\beta}' x_j - \ln z + 2\hat{\sigma}^2} \Phi\left\{\frac{1}{\hat{\sigma}}(\ln z - \hat{\beta}' x_j) - 2\hat{\sigma}\right\}$
Squared poverty gap index for household j	(A5) $\hat{P}_{2j} = \hat{P}_{1j} - \hat{\sigma} e^{\left(2\hat{\beta}' x_j - \ln z + 2\hat{\sigma}^2\right)} \Phi\left\{\frac{1}{\hat{\sigma}}(\ln z - \hat{\beta}' x_j) - 2\hat{\sigma}\right\} + \hat{\sigma} e^{\left(3\hat{\beta}' x_j - 2\ln z + 9\hat{\sigma}^2/2\right)} \Phi\left\{\frac{1}{\hat{\sigma}}(\ln z - \hat{\beta}' x_j) - 3\hat{\sigma}\right\}$

Note: The derivations of these formulae are available from the authors upon request.

References

Appleton, S. 2001. The rich are just like us, only richer: Poverty functions or consumption functions? *Journal of African Economies* 10 (4): 433–469.

Atkinson, A. B. 1989. Poverty. In *Social economics: The new Palgrave,* ed. J. Eatwell, M. Milgate, and P. Newman. New York: Norton.

Bardhan, P. K. 1984. *Land, labor and rural poverty: Essays in development economics.* New Delhi: Oxford University Press.

Banco de Moçambique. 1997. *Boletim estatístico.* Maputo: Bank of Mozambique.

Belsley, D. A., E. Kuh, and R. E. Welsch. 1980. *Regression diagnostics.* New York: John Wiley and Sons.

Cavero, W. 1998. Inquérito nacional aos agregados familiares sobre condições de vida: Relatório de missão. Instituto Nacional de Estatística, Maputo, Mozambique. Photocopy.

Datt, G., and D. Jolliffe. 1999. Determinants of poverty in Egypt: 1997. Food Consumption and Nutrition Division Discussion Paper No. 75. International Food Policy Research Institute, Washington, D.C..

Datt, G., D. Jolliffe, and M. Sharma. 2001. A profile of poverty in Egypt. *African Development Review* 13 (2): 202–237.

Deaton, A. 1997. *The analysis of household surveys: A microeconometric approach to development policy. Baltimore,* Md., U.S.A.: Johns Hopkins University Press for the World Bank.

Deaton, A., and A. Case. 1988. *Analysis of household expenditures.* Living Standards Measurement Study Working Paper No. 28. Washington, D.C.: World Bank.

Deaton, A., and M. Grosh. 2000. Consumption. In *Designing household survey questionnaires for developing countries: Lessons from 15 years of the Living Standards Measurement Study,* Vol. 1, ed. M. Grosh and P. Glewwe. Washington, D.C.: World Bank.

Deaton, A., and C. Paxson. 1998. Economies of scale, household size, and the demand for food. *Journal of Political Economy* 106 (5): 897–930.

Deaton, A., and S. Zaidi. 1999. *Guidelines for constructing consumption aggregates for welfare analysis.* Research Program in Development Studies Working Paper No. 192. Princeton, N.J.: Princeton University.

de Marrule, H., R. Benfica, P. Strasberg, D. Tschirley, and M. Weber. 1998. Algumas reflexões sobre a pobreza e as perspectivas para o crescimento do sector rural de Moçambique. *Flash* (No. 14P). Ministry of Agriculture and Fisheries, Directorate of Economics, Maputo.

Dollar, D., and A. Kraay. 2001. *Growth is good for the poor.* Policy Research Paper No. 2587. Washington, D.C.: World Bank.

________. 2002a. Spreading the wealth. *Foreign Affairs* 81 (1): 120–133.

________. 2002b. Inequality is no myth. *Foreign Affairs* 81 (4): 182–183.

Dorosh, P., S. Haggblade, H. Rajemison, B. Ralantoarilolona, and K. Simler. 1998. Structure et facteurs déterminants de la pauvreté à Madagascar. Institut National de Statistiques and Cornell Food and Nutrition Policy Program, Antananarivo, Madagascar.

Eastwood, R., and M. Lipton. 1999. The impact of changes in human fertility on poverty. *Journal of Development Studies* 36 (1): 1–30.

Foster, J., J. Greer, and E. Thorbecke. 1984. A class of decomposable poverty measures. *Econometrica* 52 (3): 761–765.

Gaiha, R. 1988. On measuring the risk of rural poverty in India. In *Rural poverty in South Asia,* ed. T. N. Srinsivasan and P. K. Bardhan. New York: Columbia University Press.

Galbraith, J. K. 2002. By the numbers. *Foreign Affairs* 81 (4): 178–183.

Gibson, J., and S. Rozelle. 2003. Poverty and access to roads in Papua New Guinea. *Economic Development and Cultural Change* 52 (1).

Glewwe, P. 1991. Investigating the determinants of household welfare in the Côte d'Ivoire. *Journal of Development Economics* 35 (2): 307–337.

Greene, W. H. 1997. *Econometric analysis.* 3rd ed. Upper Saddle River, N.J., U.S.A.: Prentice-Hall.

Greer, J., and E. Thorbecke. 1986. A methodology for measuring food poverty applied to Kenya. *Journal of Development Economics* 24 (1): 59–74.

Grootaert, C. 1997. Determinants of poverty in Côte d'Ivoire in the 1980s. *Journal of African Economies* 6 (2): 169–106.

Haddad, L., and R. Kanbur. 1990. How serious is the neglect of intrahousehold inequality? *The Economic Journal* 100 (402): 866–881.

Halvorsen, R., and R. Palmquist. 1980. The interpretation of dummy variables in semilogarithmic equations. *American Economic Review* 70 (3): 474–475.

Hardle, W. 1990. *Applied nonparametric regression.* Cambridge: Cambridge University Press.

Hausman, J. 1978. Specification tests in econometrics. *Econometrica* 46 (6): 1251–1271.

ILCA (International Livestock Center for Africa). 1990. *Livestock systems research manual.* Working Paper 1, Vol. 1. Addis Ababa.

INE (Instituto Nacional de Estatística). 1996. *Annuário estatístico 1995—Moçambique.* Maputo: Government of the Republic of Mozambique.

________. 1997. *Annuário estatístico 1996—Moçambique.* Maputo: Government of the Republic of Mozambique.

________. 1998. *Annuário estatístico 1997—Moçambique.* Maputo: Government of the Republic of Mozambique.

________. 1999. *Inquérito nacional aos agregados familiares sobre condições de vida: Resultados Gerais.* Maputo: Government of the Republic of Mozambique.

Jolliffe, D. 2002. Whose schooling matters in the determination of household income: Evidence from a developing country. *Economic Development and Cultural Change* 50 (2): 287–312.

Jolliffe, D., G. Datt, and M. Sharma. Forthcoming. Robust poverty and inequality measurement in Egypt: Correcting for spatial-price variation and sample design effects. *Review of Development Economics.*

Kennedy, P. 1981. Estimation with correctly interpreted dummy variables in semilogarithmic equations. *American Economic Review* 71 (4): 801.

Kochar, A. 1997. The savings module in the Living Standards Measurement Survey. Stanford University, Stanford, Calif., U.S.A. Photocopy.

Korn, E. L., and B. I. Graubard. 1990. Simultaneous testing of regression coefficients with complex survey data: Use of Bonferroni t statistics. *The American Statistician* 44 (4): 270–276.

Lanjouw, P. 1994. Regional poverty in Pakistan: How robust are conclusions? World Bank, Washington, D.C. Photocopy.

Lanjouw, P., and M. Ravallion. 1995. Poverty and household size. *The Economic Journal* 105 (433): 1415–1434.

Lipton, M., and M. Ravallion. 1995. Poverty and policy. In *Handbook of development economics,* Vol. 3, ed. J. Behrman and T. N. Srinivasan. Amsterdam: North-Holland.

Mole, P. N. 2000. An economic analysis of smallholder cashew development opportunities and linkages to food security in Mozambique's Northern Province of Nampula. Ph.D. diss., Department of Agricultural Economics, Michigan State University, East Lansing, Mich., U.S.A.

Mozambique, Council of Ministers. 1999. *Política nacional da população.* Maputo.

Mozambique, Ministry of Agriculture/MSU (Michigan State University). 1994. Padrões de distribuição da terra no sector familiar em Moçambique: A similaridade entre duas pesquisas distintas e as implicações para a definição de políticas. Preliminary report. Maputo.

Mozambique, Ministry of Health (Ministério de Saúde). 1991. *Tabela de composição de alimentos.* Maputo: Nutrition Section, Ministry of Health.

MPF/UEM/IFPRI (Mozambique, Ministry of Planning and Finance/Eduardo Mondlane University/ International Food Policy Research Institute). 1998. Understanding poverty and well-being in Mozambique: The first national assessment (1996–97). Washington, D.C.

Mukherjee, S., and T. Benson. 2003. The determinants of poverty in Malawi, 1998. *World Development* 31 (2): 339–358.

Newitt, M. 1995. *History of Mozambique.* Bloomington, Ind., U.S.A.: Indiana University Press.

Powell, J. L. 1994. Estimation of semi-parametric models. In *Handbook of econometrics,* Vol. 4, ed. R. F. Engel and D. L. McFadden. Amsterdam: North-Holland.

Pudney, S. 1999. On some statistical methods for modelling the incidence of poverty. *Oxford Bulletin of Economics and Statistics* 61 (3): 385–408.

Ravallion, M. 1994. *Poverty comparisons.* Chur, Switzerland: Harwood Academic Publishers.

________. 1998. *Poverty lines in theory and practice.* Living Standards Measurement Study Working Paper No. 133. Washington, D.C.: World Bank.

________. 2001. *Growth, inequality and poverty: Looking beyond averages.* Policy Research Working Paper No. 2558. Washington, D.C.: World Bank.

Ravallion, M., and B. Bidani. 1994. How robust is a poverty profile? *World Bank Economic Review* 8 (1): 75–102.

Ravallion, M., and B. Sen. 1996. When method matters: Monitoring poverty in Bangladesh. *Economic Development and Cultural Change* 44 (4): 761–792.

Reardon, T. 1997. Using evidence of household income diversification to inform study of the rural nonfarm labor market in Africa. *World Development* 25 (5): 735–747.

Rogers, W. H. 1993. Regression standard errors in clustered samples. *Stata Technical Bulletin* 13: 19–23. Reprinted in *Stata Technical Bulletin Reprints* 3: 88–94.

Sahn, D., and C. del Ninno. 1994. *Living standards and the determinants of poverty and income distribution in Maputo, Mozambique.* Working Paper 56. Ithaca, N.Y.: Cornell University Food and Nutrition Policy Program.

Schultz, T. P. 1988. Education investments and returns. In *Handbook of development economics,* Vol. 1, ed. H. Chenery and T. N. Srinivasan. Amsterdam: North-Holland Press.

Stata Corporation. 2003. *Stata statistical software: Release* 8.0. College Station, Tex., U.S.A.

Tarp, F., C. Arndt, H. T. Jensen, S. Robinson, and R. Heltberg. 2002a. *Facing the development challenge in Mozambique: An economywide perspective.* Research Report 126. Washington, D.C.: International Food Policy Research Institute.

Tarp, F., K. R. Simler, C. Matusse, R. Heltberg, and G. Dava. 2002b. The robustness of poverty profiles reconsidered. *Economic Development and Cultural Change* 51 (1): 77–108.

Tschirley, D. L., and M. T. Weber. 1994. Food security strategies under extremely adverse conditions: The determinants of household income and consumption in rural Mozambique. *World Development* 22 (2): 159–173.

USDA (United States Department of Agriculture). 1998. Composition of foods commonly eaten. Data files. Washington, D.C.

USHEW (United States Department of Health, Education, and Welfare). 1968. Nutrient content of foods commonly eaten in Africa. Washington, D.C.

West, C. E., F. Pepping, I. Scholte, W. Jansen, and H. F. F. Albers. 1987. *Food composition table for energy and eight important nutrients in foods commonly eaten in east Africa.* Wageningen, The Netherlands: Technical Center for Agriculture and Rural Cooperation of the ACP/ECP Convention of Lomé, and the Food and Nutrition Cooperation Department of Human Nutrition, Wageningen Agricultural University.

West, C. E., F. Pepping, and C. R. Temalilwa, eds. 1988. *The composition of foods commonly eaten in east Africa.* Wageningen, The Netherlands: Wageningen Agricultural University.

WHO (World Health Organization). 1985. *Energy and protein requirements.* Technical Report Series No. 724. Geneva.

Williams, R. L. 2000. A note on robust variance estimation for cluster-correlated data. *Biometrics* 56: 645–646.

World Bank. 1994a. *Poverty in Colombia.* World Bank Country Study. Washington, D.C.

________. 1994b. *Zambia poverty assessment.* Report No. 12985-ZA. Washington, D.C.

________. 1995a. *Ecuador poverty report.* World Bank Country Study. Washington, D.C.

________. 1995b. *Understanding poverty in Poland.* World Bank Country Study. Washington, D.C.

________. 1995c. *Malawi: Profile and priorities for action.* World Bank Country Study. Washington, D.C.

________. 1995d. *World development report 1995: Workers in an integrating world.* Washington, D.C.: Oxford University Press.

________. 1996a. *Hungary: Poverty and social transfers.* World Bank Country Study. Washington, D.C.

________. 1996b. *Madagascar poverty assessment.* Report No. 14044-MAG. Washington, D.C.

________. 1999. *World development report: Knowledge for development.* Washington, D.C.: Oxford University Press for the World Bank.

World Bank and Mozambique, Ministry of Agriculture and Fisheries. 1998. *Cashew production and marketing among smallholders in Mozambique: A gender-differentiated analysis based on household survey data.* Gender/Cashew Pilot Study Discussion Paper No 1. Washington, D.C.

Made in the USA
Monee, IL
08 November 2026

67984627R00063